THE FRONTIER ARMY

Frederic Remington
1909

The Frontier Army

Episodes from Dakota and the West

EDITED BY **R. ELI PAUL**

SOUTH DAKOTA
HISTORICAL SOCIETY
PRESS *Pierre*

Library of Congress Cataloging-in-Publication data is available.

This publication is funded, in part, by the Great Plains Education Foundation, Aberdeen, S.Dak.

Printed in the United States of America

The paper in this book meets the guidelines for permanence and durability of the Committee on Production Guidelines for Book Longevity of the Council on Library Resources.

Please visit our website at sdhspress.com

18 19 20 21 22 1 2 3 4 5

Cover and frontispiece: *Among the Led Horses*, 1909. Sid Richardson Museum, Fort Worth, Tex.

Design by Rich Hendel

For Tom Buecker and Jack McDermott,

whose histories of the frontier army reflected

their love of Dakota and the West.

Contents

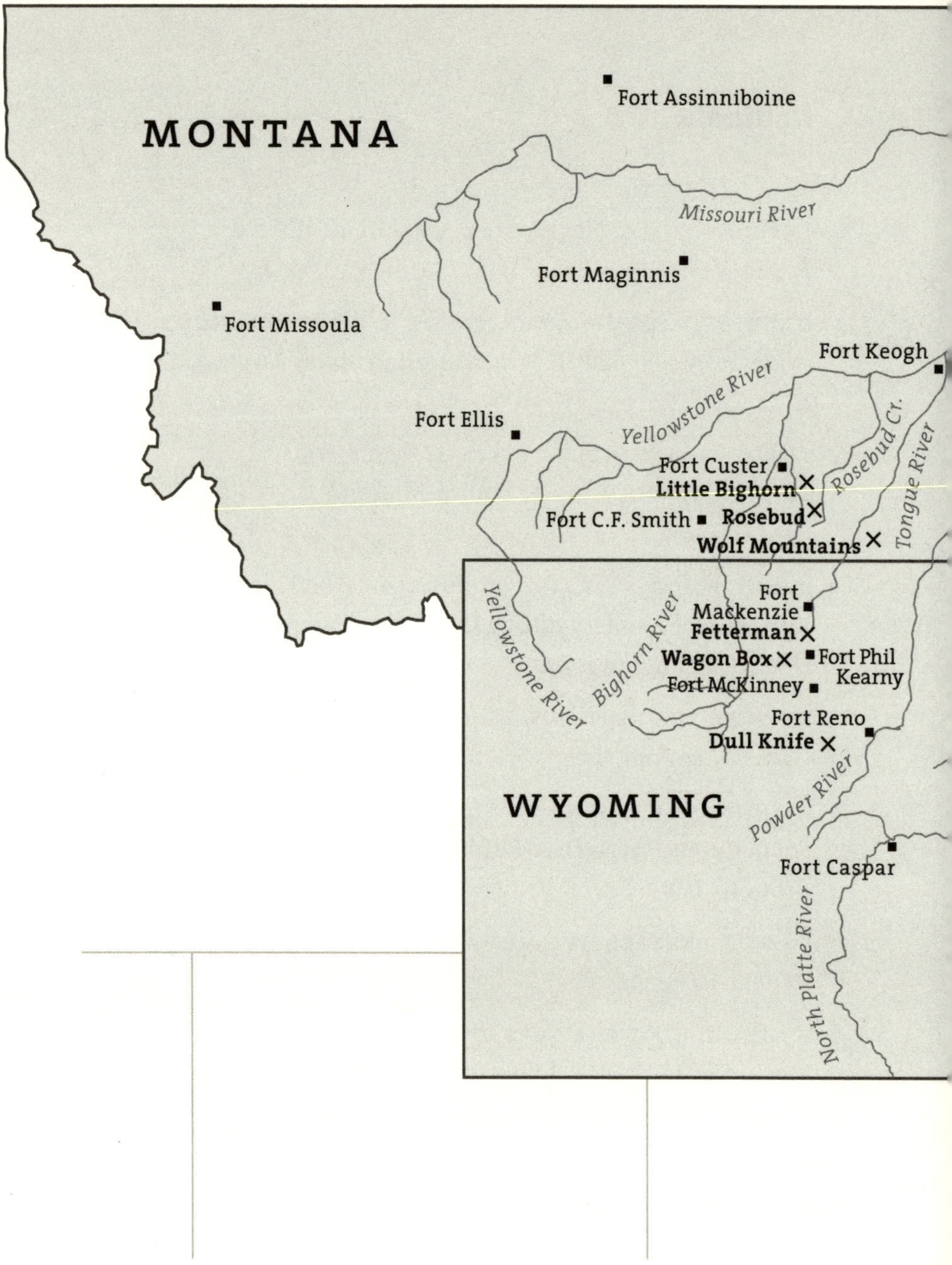

The Northern Plains of the Frontier Army

NORTH DAKOTA
Fort Buford
Fort Totten
Sheyenne River
Yellowstone River
Missouri River
Knife River
Cedar Creek
Heart River
Fort Abraham Lincoln
Cannonball River
Fort Yates
James River
Fort Sisseton
Grand River
Slim Buttes
SOUTH DAKOTA
Moreau River
Cheyenne River
Fort Meade
Fort Bennett
Fort Sully
Fort Pierre
Deadwood
Custer
GREAT SIOUX RESERVATION
White River
Wounded Knee
Missouri River
Fort Randall
Fort Fetterman
Fort Robinson
Fort Niobrara
Niobrara River
Fort Laramie
North. Platte River
NEBRASKA
Blue Water
Fort D.A. Russell
Fort Sidney
Fort McPherson
S. Platte River
Platte River
Fort Omaha
Fort Kearny

Introduction The Frontier Army Remembered

R. ELI PAUL

The American frontier army, also known as the "Old Army" or the Indian-fighting army of the mid- to late nineteenth century, drew great talents to chronicle its romantic exploits, real foibles, and legendary history. Artist Frederic Remington captured on canvas static moments in the world of the frontier regular through such masterpieces as *The Last Stand* (1891) and *Through the Smoke Sprang the Daring Soldier* (1897). Director John Ford accomplished the same in the medium of film through his own set of masterworks, particularly the "cavalry trilogy" of *Fort Apache* (1948), *She Wore a Yellow Ribbon* (1949), and *Rio Grande* (1950). Writer Charles King, less well known today but no less influential in his day, produced some sixty novels and his classic piece of personal nonfiction, *Campaigning with Crook* (1890), to create vivid, lasting word pictures of the Indian wars. A cavalcade of chroniclers of the frontier army followed in their wake, including the veteran contributors to this book as well as the two historians they honor.

This book has a dual purpose. The first is simply to present new sources and authoritative scholarship on a series of familiar topics: the history, organization, society, and culture of the frontier army; the Indian wars, particularly those conflicts between the United States government and the northern Plains tribes whose range included the Black Hills; and the critical era between 1854 and 1890, bookended by significant clashes centering around present South Dakota and its immediate neighbors. The legacy of African Americans in the Regular Army before World War I, as they made their mark on the American West, serves as a nontraditional yet apt summation.

The second reason for this volume is more personal. We lost two longtime friends and colleagues with the deaths of Thomas R. ("Tom") Buecker on 2 February 2015 and John D. ("Jack") McDermott on 31 December 2016. Buecker's curatorial stint at the Fort

Robinson Museum (1985–2011), a Pine Ridge mecca for frontier military and Indian wars history, was an especially productive time in his professional career. He authored the definitive history of Fort Robinson in two volumes as well as numerous articles on regional military history and the Plains Indian wars. McDermott followed a notable career in federal service as an independent scholar, prolific author, and most recently the biographer of Chief Red Cloud, in a book written at his Rapid City home. Both had strong roots in the state of South Dakota. McDermott grew up in Watertown and made his mark on the high school gridiron, as he often boasted, and Buecker spent the bulk of his childhood on the Thunderbird Ranch near Norbeck, as he proudly recounted.

In addition to these formative influences, it is equally important that both historians published significant works in *South Dakota History*. They were proud of these pieces and wished to be judged by these works and others. A list of their significant publications appears in the appendix. As passionate students of history to the end, always researching, writing, and sharing, both also left book-length works in progress that can be appended to this impressive list. Largely finished at the times of their deaths, Buecker's publication thoroughly covers the photographic history of Red Cloud Agency (1876–77) and McDermott's study dives deeply into the Grattan massacre and its immediate aftermath (1854–55). These subjects, along with others that attracted their scholarly attention, figure in the chapters that follow.

The contributors to this volume count themselves as only one cohort of scholars who were influenced by the duo's extensive publications, learned conversations, warm bonds, and outsized personalities. Fittingly, the group has come together to contribute articles on the subject of Buecker's and McDermott's greatest historical endeavor—the study of the American frontier army. The result is a belated but affectionate tribute to their individual careers and legacies as well as an earnest effort to further our understanding of western history.

These contributions have not been previously published. Dependent on primary sources, all have benefited from the remarkable advances in doing online military history research. What once took decades of dedicated correspondence and travel, for which McDermott was renowned, now can be significantly supplemented through a personal computer and Internet access. Incredible primary sources turn up in unlikely places, and the bibliographies of recent publications on the frontier army and the Indian wars reflect that newfound abundance of riches. The only ones not surprised are the dedicated archivists, curators, and librarians of the nation's historical repositories who have made their collections so readily accessible.

Examples of "new finds" come from the first two contributors. Marshall T. Polk, nephew of President James K. Polk, left a detailed account of the 1855 United States Army attack on a Lakota village that came as a punitive measure in response to the annihilation of Lieutenant John L. Grattan's little command near Fort Laramie the previous year. The Sioux Expedition, a topic that figured prominently in past issues of *South Dakota Historical Collections* and *South Dakota History*, involved a major early incursion through Sioux country and the Badlands. In the summer of 1855, military forces moved upriver via steamboats to garrison Fort Pierre on the Missouri, while an overland column commanded by Colonel William S. Harney simultaneously marched west along the Platte Valley route. On 3 September the column encountered the purported perpetrators of the Grattan massacre at Blue Water Creek in present western Nebraska. Immediately thereafter, Lieutenant Polk sent a letter home to Tennessee that provided frank, vivid details of the day's event as well as its immediate prelude and aftermath. His perspective on the fight came while serving as the expedition commander's aide-de-camp—literally at Harney's side. The original correspondence survives in the collections of a Tennessee repository far from South Dakota and Nebraska, missed during my earlier and larger study of the military campaign but later uncovered by serendipity during a casual Internet search.

The online abundance of nineteenth-century historic newspapers has transformed the study of the Great Sioux War. The number of eyewitness accounts discovered in newspapers published far from the action has multiplied, and new source material is continually being added. Paul Hedren adds to these new voices from the perspective of the Fourth United States Artillery, a somewhat overlooked unit of the Indian-fighting army. His annotated presentation of letters written by the officer in charge of an artillery battalion from San Francisco originally appeared in that city's *Alta California* newspaper. The correspondence describes in detail the unit's service on the gold rush trails, duty at Camp Robinson, and Black Hills experiences at the close of George Crook's 1876 summer campaign. These documents illustrate that the number of military scribes writing personal accounts of their frontier experiences—in this instance, travel to the scene of war, daily routine at guardian posts, and arduous life in the field—ordinarily exceeded the number of dutiful recorders on the formal, official side of the ledger. No narrative from the frontier military perspective can do without both types of primary documentation. The narrowly focused Sioux War reporting by Harry Cooke Cushing, Company C, Fourth Artillery, neatly complements the broader synthesis that follows it.

Doug McChristian's research has long focused on the overlooked and understudied, and it culminated recently with this generation's definitive study of soldiering on the frontier, *Regular Army O!* (2017), a fitting successor to Don Rickey's classic *Forty Miles a Day on Beans and Hay* (1963). McChristian's study of the tactical role that artillery played in the Indian wars provides a necessary corrective to understanding events largely told from the perspective of the infantry and cavalry arms of the service. The exploits of these frontier artillerymen often took place within the geography of the northern plains in the Department of Dakota and Department of the Platte. In 1876, the garrison at Fort Laramie, for example, boasted an intimidating arsenal of six artillery pieces ready for field use. One Lakota adversary was credited with aptly describing the artillery as "shoot today and kill tomorrow" (chapter 3). This story may have been long obscured because this relatively small group of field artillerymen often campaigned without their traditional armament when warm bodies, not skilled cannoneers, were needed to fill depleted ranks. The Regular Army "red legs," nicknamed for the color of the stripes on their trousers, though, did bring their deadly skills to bear at the Sioux War battles of Cedar Creek and Wolf Mountain, in the 1877 Nez Perce campaign, and most notably and tragically at Wounded Knee in 1890.

The life of the frontier soldier was not all blood and thunder, as Lori Cox-Paul shows in her chapter. Leisure time was a precious commodity that both officer and enlisted man held dear. Long, boring stretches of routine and monotonous garrison duty at isolated posts gave way to a diverse array of off-duty activities, leaving Cox-Paul to conclude half in jest that the frontier army had "no time to fight." Recreational pursuits could be socially acceptable: hunting, horseback races, gymnastics, croquet, picnics, skating, team sports, musical theater, dances, and holiday observances were all ultimately meant to steer the enlisted man away from all-to-easily-available illicit pursuits—drinking, gambling, and whoring. Fort Meade, Dakota Territory, for example, was the site of a shooting contest, an unquestionably martial event. On the other end of the spectrum, the men of Fort Randall hosted a costume ball, outdone perhaps by the Asian-themed "Mikado party" at Fort Yates near the Standing Rock Indian Reservation. The wider world considered such imaginative activities and their organizers—"isolated from society" as they were—altogether newsworthy. Recreational efforts received prominent mention in the *Army and Navy Journal* and *Army and Navy Register.* These national publications catered to the late nineteenth and early twentieth century military community and contain a wealth of information on the cultural history of the frontier army.

In addition to these military newspapers, the heavily illustrated national publications, most notably *Harper's Weekly*, offered dramatic imagery of the frontier army to go with their reams of words. No illustrator of the time was greater than Frederic Remington, "a very good friend of the army," as described by one contemporary and evaluated by Brian Dippie. Remington, whose field sketches became the basis for popular engravings and the inspiration for iconic paintings, developed into the premier "pictorial historian" of the frontier soldier. Remington was a somewhat unlikely choice for that title, an easterner through and through who never served in the military and always saw himself first as an artist, not a historian. War appalled him when he finally witnessed it up close. His collective body of work presented a rich, unvarnished, and convincing mix of observation and imagination, which endured in the public's mind more than the works of any other artist. To paraphrase Dippie, Remington's West became the "real" West, with action packed alongside the prosaic, at least until supplanted by the movies. Nevertheless, these illustrations of the Regular Army more than a century ago remain powerful, compelling images to which western historians still return. Indeed, the subject lends itself to such revisiting. Remington did so himself, never straying far afield. He returned to the topic during his entire career, maybe chastened in his later years by personal observation and acquired wisdom, but he dutifully remained a friend of the army to the end.

At one time or another the subject of the Wounded Knee Massacre, often cited as bringing the era of the Indian wars to an end, has drawn the attention of nearly all the scholars represented in this volume. Buecker and McDermott individually published source-material articles on the topic in *South Dakota History* (listed in the appendix). Jerome Greene's chapter draws upon his recent book *American Carnage* (2014), the most authoritative work on the subject, particularly the many Lakota eyewitness accounts from the 1890 massacre. The lives of the Indian survivors changed forever. Their haunting stories, passed on and collected since the time of the horrible event, have contributed immensely in transforming the accepted narrative from the initial "battles and skirmishes" storyline to one of drama, tragedy, death, and endurance. Together, the personal reminiscences and family stories of Charley Blue Arm, Dog Chief, Elks Saw Him, Chief Big Foot's brother Frog, Alice Ghost Horse, Andrew Good Thunder, Help Them, Paul High Back, Joseph Horn Cloud and his brother Iron Hail (Dewey Beard), Nellie Knife, Helena Long Bull, Medicine Woman, Edward Owl King, James Pipe on Head, Rough Feather and his wife, Spotted Horse, Peter Stand, and White Lance—all used here by Greene—form a convincing composite narrative that cannot be ignored. Even after allowing for the expected discrepancies between Indian and army participant accounts, Greene has observed, "somewhere within them lies the truth of Wounded Knee." The search for that truth deserves another look.

What is the legacy of the enlisted frontier soldier? Don Rickey, the first serious chronicler of the everyday life of the frontier regular, gave an obligatory nod to the service that "did so much to shape the development of the trans-Mississippi West."[1] But in addition to these physical accomplishments, how did that service in the American West shape our current notions of these nineteenth-century actors and how should they be remembered? And what if a significant number of those cast members were African Americans? Frank Schubert, the preeminent scholar on the buffalo soldiers of the Indian-wars era, has shown how they performed their duties and lived their lives under peculiarly trying conditions, in spite of racism and discrimination. Here, he examines their memorialization, largely an effort energized by the recent "discovery" of their history by the general public, as well as, one suspects, the modern Wyoming, South Dakota, and Nebraska communities near Forts Mackenzie, McKinney, Meade, and Robinson. Looking beyond state boundaries, Schubert provides a provocative, timely analysis of the monuments to the black soldiers who served in the Regular Army after the Civil War and before America's entry into World War I and reveals how the buffalo soldier has become embedded within modern American history and culture. A new national awareness has taken root, possibly crowding out a patch earlier seeded by Remington, Ford, and King. It is no surprise to modern scholars that African Americans have participated in major mainstream American processes. The buffalo soldiers reflect not just black history, but American history worth remembering.

The history of the American frontier army is also worthy of our continued attention, another reason why a memorial publication to remember and honor Tom Buecker and Jack McDermott is appropriate and correct. Both individuals had strong ties to the history of South Dakota and the Black Hills, its land and people. Both understood and appreciated the place and context of the topics in western history examined here. This collection of essays reflects their wide and deep interests and serves, we hope, as a worthy remembrance, tribute, and enduring legacy of their important historical work.

NOTES

1. Don Rickey, *Forty Miles a Day on Beans and Hay: The Enlisted Soldier Fighting the Indian Wars* (Norman: University of Oklahoma Press, 1963), p. 353.

1 : **Harney's Aide-de-Camp at the Blue Water Fight, 1855** A Letter by Marshall T. Polk II, United States Army

R. ELI PAUL

On 5 September 1855, two days after his United States Army command had destroyed a Lakota village, Colonel William S. Harney prepared his official report. He had discovered the camp of Chief Little Thunder of the Sicangu or Brule Lakota along the banks of Blue Water Creek a few miles away from the overland trail landmark of Ash Hollow. In the early morning of 3 September, Harney split his command, sending his mounted forces around the sleeping camp to prepare an attack from the north, while his infantry marched on the village from the south. The elaborate maneuver drew no notice from the Indians until they spotted the advancing infantrymen in the daylight.

During the commotion, as lodges were swiftly struck and the men, women, and children of the village began their retreat, Chief Little Thunder rode to Harney and his immediate staff to buy some time through a parley. Harney would have none of it. He brusquely chastised the chief, citing earlier depredations by his people against the government, and sent him off to prepare for battle. The soldiers soon commenced skirmishing from long distances, though with few initial casualties. The Indians, however, retreated inexorably north, with the infantrymen, wrote Harney, "driving the savages therefrom into the snare laid for them by the cavalry." Once the Indians encountered the horsemen, the fighting commenced in earnest, became close and fierce, and soon devolved into a rout, "completely dispersing the whole party." Hours later, after the forces of the split command regrouped, they tallied 86 Indians killed and dozens of women and children—but no men—captured, along with all the Indian lodges and their contents. These included materials considered to be proof of past transgressions—pieces of army clothing and scalps thought to be from murdered whites. Soldier losses were minimal.[1]

Commander Harney thereafter spent the second half of his triumphant report dutifully commending the officers and men of the Sioux Expedition: "I have never seen a finer military spirit displayed generally." He mentioned many of the officers by name: Lieutenant Colonel Phillip St. George Cooke led the mounted troops, whose "movement was executed in a most faultless and successful manner." Along with Cooke and his cavalry, Major Albemarle Cady, commander of the infantry companies, "carried out my instructions to them with signal alacrity, zeal, and intelligence." Captain John B. S. Todd's infantry skirmishers "opened their fire . . . in a very spirited and gallant manner." Two officers in his immediate circle shared the same praise, Captain Oscar F. Winship, Harney's chief of staff, and "Lieutenant Polk, 2nd Infantry, my aid[e]-de-camp, in conveying my orders to different portions of the command, discharged their duties with coolness, zeal, and energy."[2] And so on through the ranks.

Marshall Tate Polk II prepared his own report on the Blue Water Creek fight about the same time, but his was an unofficial account, written for a young woman he was courting, not for an army superior.[3] Both formal and informal accounts contain vivid descriptions of the fighting, colored by the expected amount of manly bravado coming from victors. Polk's more intimate account, however, presented some impolitic details on the day's events not found in Harney's or elsewhere, particularly about the fate of the vanquished. This impropriety might be expected from a young and obviously infatuated subaltern engaged in an intimate conversation.

Born in 1831 and a native Tennessean, Marshall Polk came from a distinguished family. His uncle was James K. Polk, whose inability to father children endowed Marshall with the status of the son and heir that the president never had. Such favored standing resulted in an at-large appointment to the United States Military Academy, and Polk graduated twenty-third in his West Point class of 1852. After he was assigned to the Second United States Infantry, his subsequent military career was short and undistinguished.[4]

Colonel Harney, the military expedition's chosen commander, had to put a staff together quickly in preparation for the summer's cam-

Marshall K. Polk.
findagrave.com

paign, formed as a punitive response to the so-called Grattan massacre at Fort Laramie, Nebraska Territory, in August 1854, including an aide-de-camp. Despite the differences in age and rank, it might have helped that both were Tennesseans, Jacksonian Democrats, and slaveholders. While Polk's Company C of the Second Infantry proceeded from Fort Riley, Kansas Territory, to garrison Fort Pierre on the Missouri River, the young lieutenant began his detached duties on 31 July 1855.[5]

In the days of America's antebellum army, an aide-de-camp acted as an assistant to the adjutant, in this case Captain Winship. As described in an army manual of the day, the duties of aides-de-camp were "difficult and delicate," most critically when communicating their commander's orders "verbally upon battle-fields." Moreover, "upon fields of battle they watch the movements of the enemy." Fi-

William S. Harney, commander of the Sioux Expedition of 1855–1856.
Library of Congress

nally, "their knowledge should be sufficiently comprehensive to understand the object and purpose of all orders, and also to judge in the varying circumstances of a battle-field, whether it is not necessary to modify an order when carried in person, or if there be time to return for new instructions."[6] Presumably, Lieutenant Polk brought these skills to bear at the Blue Water.

The Sioux Expedition, a force of some six hundred men, left Fort Kearny, Nebraska Territory, on 24 August 1855 and traveled west on the Platte Valley route. Many of the military participants kept journals, wrote letters, and later recorded their reminiscences of the Blue Water Creek fight that followed on 3 September. Polk's version, though, remained unpublished and largely unknown to western historians until now.[7] That is a shame, because such private, intimate accounts relating to the frontier army are relatively rare compared to the vast volume of official records, reports, and correspondence—much of it written for public consumption—generated by such historical events and government actions. Polk was not writing to an army superior or for a partisan newspaper back home or for later publication in his memoirs; he was writing only to Evelina McNeal Bills, his "own darling Eva."

THE LETTER

Camp on North Platte [River] near Ash Hollow,
September 2nd, 1855
My Dear Eva,

Night before last we stopped to camp with every prospect of having a beautiful night but, alas, for the uncertainty of all human expectations! The wind changed just about sun-down and blew stoutly from the north, and at twelve o'clock I was wakened above by the most terrific claps of thunder and the most brilliant flashes of lightning I ever saw or heard. The storm seemed to center all its strength immediately around our camp, and I expected every minute to see some of the tents struck by lightning or that the continuous flashes and crashes would cause a stampede among our animals, which would be equally as dangerous, but we escaped almost miraculously, only losing one horse. A flash struck him and crisped his mane and tore the skin around the hoofs and on his shoulders.

I have never been so much alarmed about a storm in my life and never wish to witness one similar to it again.

We reached and passed through Ash Hollow today. You know it is the great bug-bear of this road, where everyone expects to overturn wagons and meet hostile Indians. We got our train down into the Hollow all safe, but it is really the steepest hill I ever saw vehicles pass down. The Hollow is the passage through the bluffs between the north and south forks of the Platte. It is about three miles through. If the Indians only had sense enough, they could defend it against our whole army.

Just opposite and about six miles distant from us is a camp of forty lodges of Brulie [*sic*] Indians, the very fellows we are after. There are about one hundred and twenty warriors, according to the usual way of counting lodges, but we have good reason to suppose that their number is much greater. They told a "Train" today that they wanted to meet the soldiers to make peace or fight but that they preferred the former. However, their actions gave the lie to their words for they were very insolent and kicked over the coffee pot the teamsters were using. Tomorrow, I think, we will say, "The murder of our unfortunate comrades under Grattan is revenged," for we intend attacking them tonight or early in the morning, and it will not be our fault if the Indians ever forget the visit we will pay them.[8]

I don't anticipate any danger at all for it seems to me our cause is so just that their deadly arrows will pass by harmless. But, of course, I can't tell until it is all over, and, if I am hurt seriously or am killed, I hope it will be in the advance. If killed, you may rest assured that my last thought will be for my own dear Eva, the pride of my heart and my last wish for her happiness. It makes me sad to think of such things even and much more so to write about them, so I will stop until after the fight, at which time I hope to tell you all about how everybody behaved well and how I came without a scratch.

[The letter continues two days later]

Ash Hollow, Sept. 4th

Well, little Eva, the fight is over, and here I am back in camp, well and hearty, and am able to tell you myself of the bold deeds I did. The Dragoons started across the river at three o'clock yesterday morning in order to get in the rear of the Indians by daylight.

The Infantry, led by Head Quarters, started at half past four to attack the front. When they saw us coming, they struck their lodges and commenced running but did not seem afraid of us and, I've no doubt, intended to fight us at the head of the ravine. You see they did not see the Dragoons and thought we had none.

We got very uneasy about the Dragoons ourselves as we could not tell whether they could get round, as the whole country is a series of hills. By making signs we got the Chief, "Little Thunder," to come up and have a talk. When he saw the number of the Infantry, he was very anxious for peace, but the General insisted on a return for [Lieutenant John L.] Grattan's murder. After he thought the Dragoons had arrived in position, he ended the "talk." After the Chief got back to his band, we opened the ball with the minie rifle at about six hundred yards.[9]

As soon as the fight commenced, a company crossed the little stream running down the valley made by the ravine to get on the bluffs opposite and have a plunging fire on the Indians.[10] I was sent over to give them some instructions and encourage them. They went on gallantly. My horse could hardly keep his footing, but the men kept ahead of me.

When nearly on top of the bluffs, I heard a shout, and spurring up I caught a glimpse of the Dragoons after the Indians, who were making a running fight downhill. I charged downhill at an awful pace. How I did it, I don't know; the ground was so rough my horse threw his shoes and broke his hoof. When I reached the valley, the Indians were rising [ascending?] the other bluffs. Tom [Polk's horse] soon lapped the Dragoons, and taking my place by Captain [William] Steele, leading his Company [K], we went up the hill with our horses well in hand.

On reaching the top we had a good run of four or five hundred yards and the Indians before us. With a yell like so many demons, we charged, and all I saw was men, Indians, horses, and dogs all mixed up. I drew off and joined Comp[any]. E (Lieut. [Beverley H.] Robertson in command), charged another band with him, and was going to join [Lieutenant Henry] Heth, when I saw a fellow trying to shoot an old squaw. I stopped and staid [stayed] to protect her until some good man would come along. While I was with her, a dragoon came up and wished to shoot her, and I had to draw my

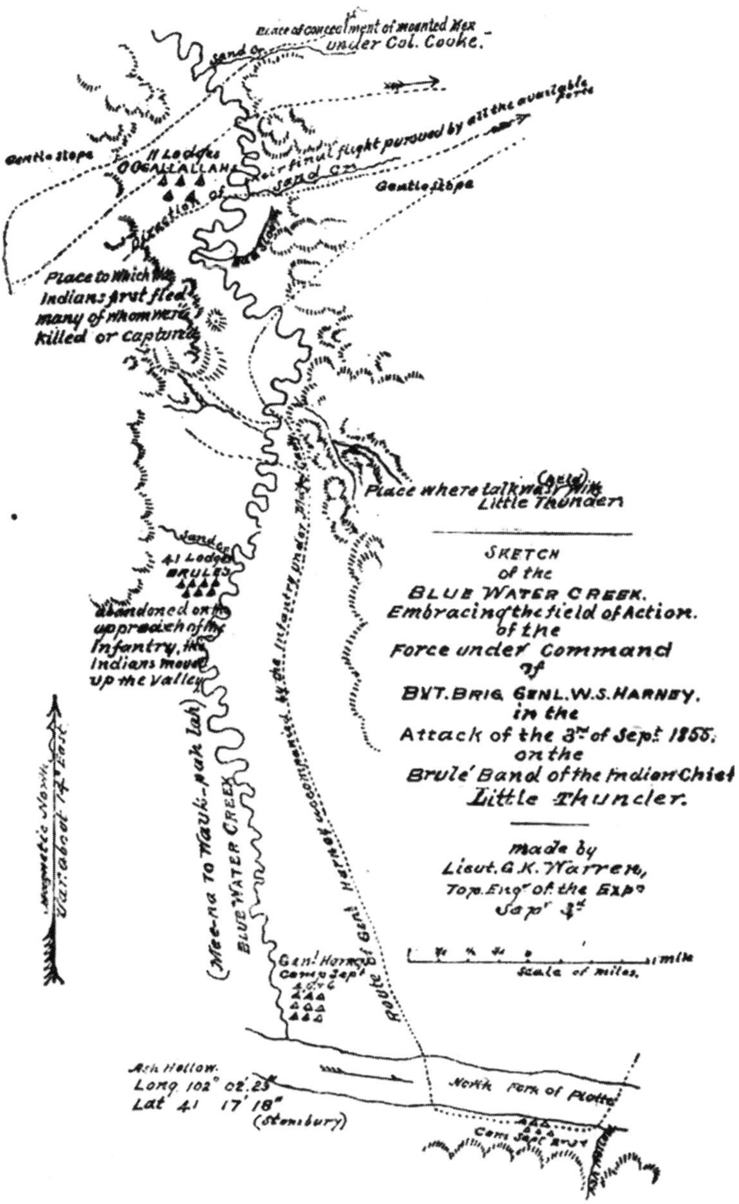

"Sketch of the Blue Water Creek" by Gouverneur K. Warren, Sept. 1855; redrawn by Robert Harvey in 1911. *Nebraska State Historical Society*

pistol and threaten to shoot him before he would desist, after calling him a coward, etc. I ordered him to join his company and fight men. As he went off, he turned and cursed me; in an instant I took aim and sent a bullet after him, and his horse jumped and saved him for the ball went up close to his head as to cause him to spring nearly out of his saddle. He thought of firing back but saw himself covered by my six-shooter and me coming closer to make the next shot sure, and he put off as hard as possible. Well, Missie, that was the only shot I fired during the fight, although I was ahead all the time, but I felt as if my place was to direct and encourage [illegible] fight. I would not have fired except to save my own life or that of another man. *Mais* [translated as "But"].

I got my old woman off to the reserve and rode over the fighting ground and picked up children.[11] The little fellows were all over the prairie, hid in the grass. A number of them were killed by reason of it; in the grass you can't tell a boy from a man, and the men fired "on sight" and frequently found themselves shooting at children. One little fellow fought like the mischief, but, as he was not more than four years old, he was soon captured.

We were extremely fortunate as only four men were killed and died last night of their wounds. We have three left wounded, two of whom are not expected to live. There are about fifty prisoners, all women and children. Not a man was taken prisoner. The Indians lost between forty and fifty warriors, besides women and children killed in the melee. The chief was killed, and the voice of "Little Thunder" will no more rattle in the council of his tribe.[12] The women and children killed was accidental.[13] A man was killed by a shot from out a ravine, and the men exasperated fired upon a mass of men, women, and children, killing between twenty and thirty of them.[14]

As we expected, we found another village above, and the number of warriors in all was about two hundred and fifty. All their goods are in our hands and will be destroyed, it is supposed.

I could tell you of scenes I have witnessed that would shock you, but it makes me sick to recall them to myself, one thing I saw which will never be erased from my memory.

This fight has commenced what we all think will be a bloody war, and it has decided General Harney to keep all out here this winter so as to be able to make [a] winter campaign. It will be awful duty, and we will lose more men by hardship than battle, but at the same time it is the most successful plan to terminate the war. The decision is disagreeable to all but especially so to me, and my only hope is that he may make his own headquarters at Fort Riley. It will be impossible for me to leave while he is here.

After the fighting was over, we all went to pillaging, that is, picking up robes, saddle ornaments, pipes, etc. My share is the great medicine pipe with all its trappings and a scalp lock, only the hair, and they have dyed that red; it (the bundle) is a real curiosity, and I intend preserving it. I also have an ornamented bag with a thousand and one things in it.[15]

This band certainly murdered the mail party for in their camp and on their persons we found papers, such as letters, contracts, etc., and above all a picture rudely made but representing the mail party as they appeared when attacked; we also have several letters written from the states to friends in the far west. In their caricatures they have made the soldiers with high-heeled boots, spurs, and very large moustaches; one old fellow is represented with a red dressing gown on, both hands raised high up, and a very ludicrous expression of fright and surprise upon his face; no doubt the redskins had many a hearty laugh over the pictures, but they have paid dearly for their mirth.[16]

You no doubt will be shocked at my mentioning women having been killed, but think that they ride and dress just like the men, and it is hard to tell the difference without being very near them. Besides they are dangerous, as one of our poor fellows could prove if he was alive. He was a bold fellow and had chased an Indian some time but upon discovering it was a squaw rode by her without firing. He had hardly passed when she shot him through with an arrow.

Those taken prisoners seem to take things very coolly. Some of them went to making moccasins ten minutes after being captured, and the children went to playing as if in their own lodges. Heth and myself found one little fellow way out by himself, and, when I dismounted and held my hand to him, he came and leaned his head against me. A man brought him to me in camp.

But now I will tell you of the boldest feat I performed during the action, and it affords me the more pleasure to relate it, as it is innocent and reflects credit on my horse. In the charge Lieut. [Nathan A. M.] Dudley tried to pass across in front of us, but being on a pony he was not quite quick enough. Tom got nearly on him, but instead of running against he raised and jumped over the pony just behind Dudley! Now isn't it a great thing? Dudley told me of it afterwards for I don't remember it; he says he expected to be knocked off but was greatly relieved when Tom cleared his horse behind him.[17] I use to think a man could not ride without sitting well in the saddle, but it is different now for I verily believe that sometimes only my spurs were touching the horse. I am afraid I will make my horse as big a bug-bear to you as I did the buffalo [a letter of 22 August 1855 describing a bison hunt stated perhaps sheepishly, "I have at last covered myself with glory by killing a fine buffalo cow"]. But remember that out here a man's chance of having an original thought is very small, and he must take any subject and manufacture it into words.

The wolves were just now howling tattoo all round camp, and, as it is past ten o'clock, I will spare you for the rest of the evening; so angels guard you, little Pet.

Sept. 6th, 1855

The Express will start in a short time, so I will finish my letter and have it ready to go off. The General has concluded to leave one company of Infantry with the wounded and prisoners at this place to protect them. He is causing a temporary fort [Fort Grattan] to be thrown up; how long they will remain here is not known, probably until November or December.

The affair is called the "Battle of the Blue Water"; to let you see the appropriateness of the name I will describe the grounds. From the Platte the[re] is a small valley reaching to the Bluffs, maybe a mile and three quarters wide. Then the Bluffs rise, and from these latter there comes a beautiful little stream to empty into the main river. On the right bank of this creek the Bluffs extend clear down to the Platte, but on either bank is a small rich valley, ending in a range of hills at the upper end. In this valley was [were] the Indians, the Infantry, between them and the Platte, the Dragoons between them and the range of hills mentioned. Being in this fix they tried to mount the hills on the right bank of the creek but were met and turned by a portion of the Infantry and mounted forces and were compelled to retreat by the hills on the left bank of the creek. This

The winding Blue Water Creek, Garden County, Nebraska, 1929.
Nebraska State Historical Society

forced direction threw them in the path of Steele's and Robertson's companies of Dragoons [K and E], who charged them with great effect, killing quite a large number. It was beautifully done, although I say it. The creek is called "Minie Whack Palah" [Mini Wakpala in the Lakota language] or "Blue Water."

When those nice young men are floating round you and swearing fidelity, you must not believe them for they have no excuse to be otherwise; they have you with them, constantly in their sight, and their constancy is more the result of compulsion than their own free will, but with me it is different. I cannot hear your dear voice, I cannot see the sparkle of your eye, nor feel the influence of your sweet smile. I cannot even receive pleasure from your letters for they never reach me, but still I am faithful. Your image alone fills my heart. All I live for is the hope of again joining you and finding my own darling Eva unchanged. It is, I know, almost sacriledge [*sic*] to mention the word change, but I don't believe you can change. You are too good to think of such a thing, and, if you will only picture me way out here by myself, you will send those fellows about their business.

Give my love to all. Your own, Marshall

EPILOGUE

The expedition marched to Fort Laramie and then pushed on through the Badlands to Fort Pierre on the Missouri River. In a 13 October 1855 letter written a hundred miles from the post, Polk implored Eva, "I have carried your dagguerreotype [*sic*] next to my heart. I have dreamed and talked of nothing but you, and now won't you reward me?" She did. Polk received new orders, left for St. Louis in late October, and returned to Tennessee, where he married her on 10 January 1856.[18] The young lieutenant resigned from the United States Army on 10 April and oversaw his Bolivar plantation until the Civil War, when he took up arms enthusiastically for the Confederacy.[19] Polk made the same choice as Heth, Robertson, and Steele, other former West Pointers and fellow alumni of the Sioux Expedition who figured into his correspondence with Evelina Bills.

Polk may have made as little impact during the Civil War as he did in the First Sioux War. For example, buried in his commander's report for the 1862 Battle of Shiloh was an unintentionally ironic (to the modern reader) statement: "And here also fell many officers of lesser grade, among them the gallant Captain Marshall T. Polk of Polk's battery, who lost a leg, as well as a large number of his men."[20] Not mentioned was Polk's capture by Union forces and the subsequent intercession of his Aunt Sally, the former President Polk's widow, who had the injured prisoner removed to her care. Polk recovered so well that he was later exchanged, returned to duty, and served through the remainder of the war.[21]

Polk again returned to Bolivar and a gentleman's life, eventually becoming state treasurer for Tennessee. His public service career ended badly, though, with his 1883 trial and guilty verdict for embezzling $400,000 in state funds, an enormous sum for the time and a scandal that drew national attention. His legal woes evaporated with his convenient death from natural causes in 1884. Eva survived him and lived until 1926.[22]

NOTES

1. "Report of General Harney, Commander of the Sioux Expedition, September 5, 1855," *Senate Executive Documents*, 34th U.S. Cong., 1st and 2nd sess., 1855–56, No. 1, Serial 811. For a lengthy description of Ash Hollow in present Garden County, Nebraska, *see* Merrill J. Mattes, *The Great Platte River Road: The Covered Wagon Mainline via Fort Kearny to Fort Laramie* (Lincoln: Nebraska State Historical Society, 1969), chap. 9. For more on the Blue Water fight, *see* R. Eli Paul, *Blue Water Creek and the First Sioux War, 1854–56* (Norman: University of Oklahoma Press, 2004), chap. 6.

2. "Report of General Harney."

3. This particular original letter, along with a typescript transcription by a family member, is found in the Marshall Tate Polk Family Papers, 1826–1981, a collection in the Tennessee State Library and Archives, Nashville. I wish to thank that organization's professional staff members for their help in making this collection readily accessible to researchers, particularly Jay Richiuso, assistant director for Manuscript Services.

4. John S. Jenkins, *James Knox Polk and a History of His Administration, Embracing the Annexation of Texas, the Difficulties with Mexico, the Settlement of the Oregon Question, and Other Important Events* (Auburn and Buffalo, N.Y.: John E. Beardsley, 1850), p. 330; George W. Cullum, *Biographical Register of the Officers and Graduates of the U.S. Military Academy at West Point, N.Y., from Its Establishment in 1802 to 1890*, 3 vols. (Boston: Houghton, Mifflin, 1891), 2:493–94, no. 1558.

5. Paul, *Blue Water Creek*, pp. 66, 68; Post Return, Fort Riley, Kans. Terr., May 1855, Returns from U.S. Military Posts, 1800–1916, Records of the Adjutant General's Office, Record Group (RG) 94, National Archives and Records Administration (NARA), Washington, D.C.; Officers of the Department Staff, present and absent, accounted for by name, Field Returns of the Sioux Expedition, Aug. 1855, Returns of Expeditions, RG 94, NARA.

6. H[enry]. L[ee]. Scott, *Military Dictionary: Comprising Technical Definitions, Information on Raising and Keeping Troops, Actual Service, Including Makeshifts and Improved Materiél, and Law Government, Regulation, and Administration Relating to Land Forces* (New York: D. Van Nostrand, 1864), p. 21.

7. Polk's account did not appear in a listing of participant accounts of the Blue Water fight compiled in Paul, *Blue Water Creek*, pp. 167–79; nor was it cited—or he even mentioned—in another book-length study, Paul N. Beck's *The First Sioux War: The Grattan Fight and Blue Water Creek, 1854–1856* (Lanham, Md.: University Press of America, 2004).

8. Lieutenant Gouverneur K. Warren of the Topographical Engineers later made an exact count, listing on a map forty-one lodges of Brules plus eleven more of the Oglala Lakota tribe that were not discovered until after the fight commenced.

James A. Hanson, *Little Chief's Gatherings: The Smithsonian Institution's G. K. Warren 1855–1856 Plains Indian Collection and the New York State Library's 1855–1857 Warren Expeditions Journals* (Chadron, Nebr.: Fur Press, 1996), p. 105. Warren's map of the battlefield is a crucial source for following and understanding the course of the action on 3 September. Regarding population estimates, a standard rule of thumb of the day figured three men of fighting age per Plains Indian lodge. R. Eli Paul, "Counting Indians," *Wild West* 18 (Dec. 2005): 27. Regarding supposed Indian insolence to overland travelers, a literate teamster confirmed and later recorded this incident. William Chandless, *A Visit to Salt Lake: Being a Journey across the Plains and a Residence in the Mormon Settlements at Utah* (London: Smith, Elder, and Co., 1857), pp. 74–75.

9. The army's use of the innovative and more deadly "long-range rifle" on the Sioux Expedition is discussed in Paul, *Blue Water Creek*, pp. 50–53, 95–99.

10. These Sixth Infantrymen were probably members of Company A, commanded by Captain Todd. Ibid., p. 95.

11. "Reserve" may refer to where the two companies of Sixth Infantry were held in reserve. Ibid.

12. Later it was learned that Little Thunder had narrowly survived the fight. James Bordeaux, a Fort Laramie trader, said that Little Thunder had been "knocked off his horse by a ball which struck his butcher knife." "Ranger," Laramie Bridge, Nebr. Terr., 7 Sept. 1855, to Thom. J. Keenan, editor, *Pittsburg Union* (Pittsburg[h], Pa.), reprinted in *Bedford Gazette* (Bedford, Pa.), 2 Nov. 1855.

13. "Accidental" killing of noncombatants was contradicted by American Indian testimony, in particular by Cokawin, a Lakota woman who was intentionally shot down but survived to tell her story to a later generation. Susan Bordeaux Bettelyoun and Josephine Waggoner, *With My Own Eyes: A Lakota Woman Tells Her People's History*, edited by Emily Levine (Lincoln: University of Nebraska Press, 1998), pp. 57–58, 62–64.

14. Polk may be describing a tragic episode when a remnant group of fleeing Indians sought shelter in a rock overhang, put up resistance against the soldiers, and were indiscriminately shot until only the surviving women and children surrendered. Paul, *Blue Water Creek*, p. 104.

15. Today's whereabouts of the relics that Polk picked up are unknown, but Lieutenant Warren's relics became part of the Plains Indian collections of the National Museum of Natural History, Smithsonian Institution. Ibid., p. 108; Hanson, *Little Chief's Gatherings.*

16. The "one old fellow" may have been Charles A. Kinkead, the lone survivor of the 13 November 1854 attack on the United States mail. Lakota raiders, including the warrior Spotted Tail, carried out this act of vengeance for the killing of Chief Conquering Bear by Grattan on the overland trail east of Fort Laramie. Spotted Tail

fought bravely at the Blue Water fight. "The Indian Murder Near Fort Laramie," *North American and United States Gazette* (Philadelphia, Pa.), 18 Dec. 1854, in John D. McDermott, R. Eli Paul, and Sandra J. Lowry, eds., *All Because of a Mormon Cow: Historical Accounts of the Grattan Massacre, 1854–1855* (Norman: University of Oklahoma Press, 2018), pp. 162–65; Paul, *Blue Water Creek*, pp. 32–33, 78–79, 105.

17. Lieutenant Dudley served in Heth's Tenth Infantry company, which was mounted on ponies and used as cavalry on the expedition. Reminiscing a half-century later, he made no mention of Polk's equestrian feat. R. Eli Paul, ed., "Battle of Ash Hollow: The 1909–1910 Recollections of General N. A. M. Dudley," *Nebraska History* 62 (Fall 1981): 373–99.

18. Polk letter to Eva, 13 Oct. 1855, Marshall Tate Polk Family Papers, 1826–1981; Field Returns of the Sioux Expedition, Oct. 1855; Evelyn McNeal Polk Eldred, "Memoir of Evelina McNeal Bills Polk" (1919), sites.google.com/site/historicbolivartn/gone-but-not-forgotten/evelina-mcneal-bills-polk-memoir (hereafter "Polk Memoir").

19. Cullum, *Biographical Register*, 2:493.

20. S. L., "The Battle of Shiloh: General [Leonidas] Polk's Official Report, Achievements of Tennesseans," Richmond correspondence of the *Knoxville Register*, reprinted in *Memphis Daily Appeal*, 23 Mar. 1863.

21. "Polk Memoir."

22. Ibid.; "Polk! Full Particulars of His Arrest," *Public Ledger* (Memphis), 11 Jan. 1883; "Death of Ex-Treasurer Polk: The Tennessee Defaulter Expires Suddenly; His Career and Crime," *New York Times*, 1 Mar. 1884; "Marshall T. Polk" obituary, in *15th Annual Reunion of the Association of the Graduates of the United States Military Academy, at West Point, New York, June 13, 1884* (E. Saginaw, Mich.: Courier Printing Co.), pp. 101–2.

2 : The Fourth United States Artillery and the Great Sioux War Source Material

PAUL L. HEDREN

In the depths of the Great Sioux War, General William Tecumseh Sherman expressed matters succinctly and rather candidly in his annual report to the secretary of war, recognizing that the Sioux campaign "had been planned on wrong premises." Trying in part to explain why Custer and five companies of the Seventh Cavalry were dead, Sherman acknowledged that his troops faced an enemy numbering far more than the 500 to 800 so-called Northern Indians that had been foretold at the start of the war. Instead, the army confronted not just those northern traditionalists but countless agency people as well, "who had gone out to help their friends in a fight."[1]

At the ebb of a miserable summer campaign, Alfred H. Terry and George Crook, the army's field generals in this war, sought reinforcements. Philip H. Sheridan, William Tecumseh Sherman's strategist for the war, responded quickly, deploying to the northern plains the Fifth Cavalry and Fifth Infantry from the Department of the Missouri and the Twenty-Second Infantry from the Division of the Atlantic. Sheridan soon redoubled those transfers by also sending to the war zone elements of the Fourth Cavalry and Eleventh Infantry, again from the Department of the Missouri. Those departures from the central and southern plains seriously weakened the strengths and capabilities of surviving garrisons, so Sheridan scattered companies of artillery drawn from the First, Second, and Third Regiments and normally quartered on the Atlantic and Gulf seaboards to those inland posts. He also dispatched a four-company battalion of the Fourth Artillery from California directly to Nebraska and the Sioux war. Normalcy in troop dispositions in America's small and frightfully scattered army would not return for a very long while.[2]

The four Fourth Artillery companies (or batteries as they were also commonly known) dispatched to the Sioux war were drawn from San Francisco Bay area posts: C from the Presidio of San Francisco, F from Point San José, and H and K from Alcatraz Island. The Fourth Artillery had served in California and Alaska since the fall of 1872. Like all artillery regiments, the Fourth ordinarily served heavy guns mounted in massive brick coastal fortifications. An exception in this regiment was Company B, designated a light battery and serving three-inch ordnance rifles and 12-pounder Napoleon guns. Half of the regiment, including Company K, had served in California's Modoc Indian War in 1873, a disastrous conflict with many casualties, including Brigadier General Edward R. S. Canby, killed outright by Indians. Of the six companies deployed to the Modoc War, one served small Coehorn mortars, B served as cavalry mounted on the battery's horses, and the others acted as infantry, a role imitated by the four companies dispatched to the Sioux war.[3]

Thirteen officers participated in the Sioux campaign, including assistant surgeon and First Lieutenant Curtis E. Price, the physician assigned to the battalion. Eight were West Point graduates and six were veterans of the Civil War. Only four, Lieutenants Sydney W. Taylor of Company C, Walter Howe and George G. Greenough of Company K, and Harry R. Anderson of Company H, had previously experienced an Indian campaign, all in the Modoc War. The battalion commander, Captain Joseph B. Campbell, who also led Company F during the five-month deployment, was the senior officer present for duty. Other company commanders included Captains Harry C. Cushing (C) and Frank G. Smith (H), and, consecutively, Howe and Greenough (K). Campbell's first lieutenant in Company F, Albert S. Cummins, served additionally as battalion adjutant.[4]

The apparently self-appointed and lone chronicler of the Fourth Artillery's deployment to the Great Sioux War was thirty-five-year-old Harry Cooke Cushing of Company C. Born in Maryland but hailing from Rhode Island, Cushing came from a family with a strong military heritage. His father, George, served as a captain with Rhode Island volunteers during the Civil War. His brother Samuel graduated from West Point in 1860 and served with the Second United

States Infantry and Subsistence Department in the war and afterward, including a stint in Omaha in 1866–67 as chief of commissary for the Department of the Platte. A Brown University student before the Civil War, Harry also saw extensive service during the conflict, initially in the enlisted ranks with the First Rhode Island Light Artillery and then as a commissioned officer in the Fourth United States Artillery. Cushing was engaged at Winchester, Cedar Mountain, Antietam, Murfreesboro, Chickamauga, and Chattanooga and served finally with Sheridan in the Shenandoah Valley campaign until near the war's end. He was breveted three times for meritorious service in the Civil War, including to the grade of major, and remained with the Fourth Artillery after the war, promoted to captain in August 1871.[5]

Cushing's Sioux war reporting came in the form of letters to the *Daily Alta California* of San Francisco, one of California's most respected and widely read newspapers. The paper was already featuring occasional Sioux war stories provided by another correspondent, Joe Wasson, and had regular war-related columns from other sources as well, reporting and commenting on happenings from the northern plains in what was proving to be a fateful Indian war. News of the Fourth Artillery's deployment appeared twice in the *Alta California* on 12 August. The paper noted that the battalion would travel by rail to Cheyenne, Wyoming, and was ultimately bound for the Spotted Tail and Red Cloud agencies in Nebraska, "from which troops have already been withdrawn for the front." The paper also noted that four companies of the First Cavalry were ordered to hold themselves in readiness for deployment to the Department of the Platte. That deployment order was never issued, however. The men of the Fourth Artillery were given but one day to put themselves in readiness and then embarked for the plains.[6]

In all, the *Daily Alta California* printed three long, breezy letters from Cushing, variously chronicling the travels of the battalion across California, northern Nevada, and southern Wyoming; the travails of marching as infantry overland from Cheyenne to Fort Laramie and Camp Robinson, their final destination; and the burdens of escort duty, itself a narrative unlike anything in the enormous body of Great Sioux War literature. At Camp Robinson, the artillerymen fell into a relatively ordinary routine associated with camp life, though Cushing wrote at length about the hustle evident at the post and nearby Red Cloud Agency. The comings and goings of agency Indians and army commands held everyone's rapt attention. While at Camp Robinson, Campbell's battalion constructed and occupied an unpretentious hovel of log huts and dugouts called Camp Canby, honoring the deceased General Canby. It was located on the north bank of the White River about midway between the post and Red Cloud Agency, each a mile or so away. A similar sprawl nearby called Camp Custer housed transient cavalry troops commanded by Colonel Ranald S. Mackenzie, also newly arrived from the Indian Territory. With these additional artillery and cavalry contingents and other troops deployed from within the Department of the Platte, plus the local garrison, Cushing noted that eighteen companies of soldiers were present for duty at or near Camp Robinson. That was the largest troop concentration thus far on the northern plains and a certain reflection of Sheridan's resolve to flood Sioux Country with as many troops as necessary to hasten the conclusion of the Great Sioux War.[7]

In addition to engaging in the sometimes turbulent day-to-day affairs of Camp Robinson and Red Cloud Agency (described in Cushing's second letter), the battalion's singular noteworthy undertaking that early fall was escorting a substantial supply train northward through the Black Hills bound for General Crook's campaign-weary column, which was slowly snaking its way southward through the Black Hills after months in the field. Crook's troops had only barely survived an exhausting, debilitating march from the Yellowstone River in Montana to the Black Hills, coming by way of the Slim Buttes in western Dakota and a sharp Indian fight there on 9–10 September. Three of the four artillery companies of the escort were led by Captain Smith. Campbell and Company F remained at Camp Canby. Crook, meanwhile, having been summoned to Fort Laramie by General Sheridan to commence planning yet another movement against the Sioux and advancing ahead of his own column, ran headlong into Smith's caravan about midway between Deadwood and Custer City. Cushing's description of a puzzlingly attired, taciturn General Crook adds measurably to our sense of this prominent Indian fighter. Crook and his escort paused long enough with the artillerymen to partake of a noon meal.[8]

Crook directed Smith to unload his wagons at Box Elder Creek, leave a company behind to guard the supplies, and return the empty wagons to Camp Robinson. Wagon transportation in the Department of the Platte was in short supply this season, and Crook probably already anticipated the resumption of campaigning later that fall. First Lieutenant Howe and Company K remained at Box Elder Creek and were soon encountered by the weary column, now commanded by Colonel Wesley Merritt, as it wended its way southward from Deadwood. The artillerymen were "eagerly greeted," remembered First Lieutenant Charles King of the Fifth Cavalry, who was struck by the glaring disparities between the troops, the "spruce artillerymen fresh from their casemates on the seaboard, who looked upon our rags with undisguised astonishment." More important were the stockpiled provisions, including measures of oats and corn distributed to emaciated animals. "It was only a bite for the poor creatures," King recalled, "and their eyes begged wistfully for more." It had been a grueling campaign, and the men and animals of this column were thoroughly consumed.[9]

Sheridan, Crook, and Mackenzie indeed planned another field movement at Fort Laramie that was largely organized at Camp Robinson and eventually embarked from Fort Fetterman, Wyoming, on 14 November. It was Crook's largest and most complex Sioux war orchestration yet, featuring eleven companies of cavalry, eleven companies of infantry, and Captain Campbell's four-company artillery battalion. The formally anointed Powder River Expedition was an eventful campaign lasting a month and a half. Crook's cavalry battalion led by Mackenzie struck a devastating blow on a Northern Cheyenne village nestled in a canyon of the Red Fork of the Powder River in the southern Big Horn Mountains. The 25 November battle only involved Crook's cavalry, however; his infantry and artillery troops were held in reserve for support as needed. The expedition closed operations at the end of December, successful at Red Fork but by then done in by the weather.[10]

Cushing seems not to have penned any additional letters for *Alta California* from the Sioux war. His final communiqué was datelined from Deadwood and printed in the newspaper on 2 October. The Fourth Artillery battalion's return to San Francisco was quietly noted in the *Alta California*: "Major Cushing, Major Campbell, and their associate officers congratulate themselves on again being within the sound of the church-going bells, and enjoying a climate that does not

First Lieutenant Albert S. Cummins of Company F, seen here as a West Point cadet in 1873. *Paul Hedren Collection*

require a double thickness of furs to keep the person from freezing." Several days earlier Captain Smith was noted in an Omaha newspaper. He was just in from Cheyenne and eastbound for Saint Paul, Minnesota, anxious to visit family. Said the *Omaha Bee*: "He said he had not slept between sheets for over four months until he struck the Pullman cars on the Union Pacific. At one time during the expedition, the cold was so intense that the mercury froze, and the army had nothing to burn but sage-brush." A quiet but meaningful tribute to these artillery troops came from Ranald Mackenzie, commanding the cavalry in the Wyoming campaign. Responding to a puzzling remark about "red-legged" infantry, he replied that he had "never seen a better battalion of foot troops than Campbell's, or one better commanded."[11]

The principal officers in this unique deployment of the Fourth Artillery enjoyed long and fulfilling Regular Army careers following the Great Sioux War. Holding the rank of colonel, Walter Howe commanded troops in the Philippine Insurrection; in 1905, he organized and commanded the first Provisional Regiment of Field Artillery at Fort Sill. He reached the grade of brigadier general in 1910 and was the last member of his West Point class on the army's active list when he retired that year.[12] George Greenough and Frank Smith both also reached the grade of colonel and commanded troops in the Philippines, retiring early in the twentieth century as brigadier generals.[13] Battalion commander Joseph Campbell, severely wounded and breveted for heroics at Antietam, who served twice as an instructor at the Artillery School at Fort Monroe, died in service in 1891 with the rank of major, Second Artillery.[14] Campbell's adjutant, Albert Cummins, likewise enjoyed a long career, retiring in 1908 as a colonel of the Coast Artillery Corps. He was recalled to active duty to command coastal defenses in the Puget Sound in 1917–18.[15] Sioux war correspondent Harry Cushing returned to the field against Indians twice more, in 1877 against the Nez Perces in Idaho and Montana and briefly in 1881 against Apaches in Arizona. He retired in 1895 owing to disability, holding the rank of major. His vibrant letters from the Great Sioux War burnished a long, eventful, and accomplished career.

Daily Alta California, August 19, 1876

EN ROUTE TO THE FRONT

Special to the Alta

Sleeping Car "Denver," U.P.R.R., Near Point of Rocks, Wyoming Territory, August 15, 1876.

This is the fete day of the great Napoleon, and if it is permitted to the departed to look down upon the affairs of the sublunary sphere, that great warrior must experience a feeling of surprise at seeing a body of troops, which left San Francisco on the evening of the 12th of August, at a point over 1200 miles from their starting place, and bowling along toward their objective point at the rate of twenty miles an hour. The insignificant Captain of Artillery, who makes the above reflections, is pursuing the path to fame in a manner more comfortable and attended with more luxury than if he were provided with the sumptuous campaign carriage which astonished the English officers who captured it from the great Napoleon aforesaid at the Battle of Waterloo. He soothes the acerbities of war on a double lower berth; is ministered to by a correct and unimpeachable American gentlemen of African descent; indites this communication on a broad and comfortable table, and surveys his war-worn frame in a dozen mirrors. He announces at night that he will take his breakfast at a point two or three hundred miles away, and retired to rest on a hair mattress, after so declaring, with the firm belief that the preliminaries of the breakfast are at that instant being arranged. The next morning he rises, and after putting on his shoes, which shine like the face of the newly-washed school-boy, he eats his ante-prandial peaches and grapes in the midst of the great American Desert, and looking at this watch, d——ns the Union Pacific Railroad Company because it is ten minutes late in a stretch of seventy leagues.

The great Napoleon, considering these wonders, resolves to investigate this affair, and discovers that an American General, sitting in his office at Washington, orders on the 10th of August, another American General sitting in his office at San Francisco, three thousand miles away, to immediately dispatch four companies of artillery to Cheyenne, 1500 miles from each. The result of which is that the great Napoleon observes at 11 A.M., on his fete day, August 15th, the four companies thus ordered booming along at twenty miles an hour at a point only twenty miles distant from the aforesaid Cheyenne. Upon this, the great Napoleon seeks Alexander, Hannibal, and Caesar, who are reviewing their wonderful achievements to the Baron Jomini in the Elysian Fields, and, inspired with American ideas, vents his admiration in American phraseology, with the remark that "this is h——." Seriously speaking, when one comes to consider that this battalion is 1300 miles from its regular post, under orders emanating from a General 3000 miles away given on the 10th of August, a modern skeptic might, with justice, say that the causing of the sun to stand still by Joshua was not such great shakes after all. The operations of nature have not been interfered with by us as was the case with Joshua. The sun has been allowed to roll on. He has attended to business while we have anticipated him. The watches of this command have been undergoing the same tribulations of that of Mark Twain's young friend.

There is not very much to record of interest. The main topics have been where we should get breakfast and supper, and where we should meet the overland train. The scribbling of postal cards has been simply immense. We have no doubt that the overland train has been delayed on account of the extra weight.

At Terrace,[16] a communicative citizen in a hickory shirt informed us that Pocatello, an Indian, with a reputation for peacefulness far below the average, had been seeking to replenish his stores of ammunition. This genial savage is, we believe, a model Lo, and we left Terrace with the belief that he was preparing to cause a further depletion of the San Francisco garrison.

Further on, at Ogden, we learned that a dispatch had been received, announcing that Crook had defeated the Sioux. We trust it may be so.[17]

A definite idea as to where we are going, it does not exist. The popular idea now is that we are to go to Cheyenne, and there be placed under the orders of Colonel Mackenzie, of the Fourth Cavalry, who is now there. This officer having had a large experience with the Comanches and Kiowas in Texas, it is supposed has been entrusted with the task of running the Agencies in this Department, and we are to be under his orders for that service. He is an excellent officer, and no one would be disappointed if we were put under his orders. The health of the command is good, and nothing has occurred to interrupt harmony. The weather is delightful and cool.

Mr. Bird-o'-Freedom Sawin's remark about the country around Saltille might be well applied to the country through which we are now traveling: "This here's about the meanest place a skunk might well diskiver." Interminable stretches of barren hills, permeated with rain-washed gullies, and bristling with sage-brush, greet the eye in every direction. The only signs of an advanced civilization, which it is presumed a Centennial year should afford, are the recurring telegraph poles which jump past us with a tiresome monotony. While smoking the post-prandial cigar, I endeavored to count them, and even formed a laudable intention of doing it until I got to Cheyenne. But happening to recollect that I belonged to a scientific corps, I counted the number in a mile, and as soon as I get to where I can get at a reliable work on mathematics propose to work out the answer for the whole distance by logarithms. The telegraphic wires are not regarded with as much favor as they were, for the impression is strong that but for the absurd experiments of Morse, we might have been enjoying the quiet of a comfortable artillery home, and the redoubtable Sitting Bull careering over the Bad Lands oblivious of the existence of the Fourth Artillery. We agree with Ruskin that there are too many inventions.[18] However, it is business, and we try to make it pleasure.

We are getting along as I pencil these remarks; occasionally we pass a group of Mongolian gentlemen engaged in repairing the road. When Sitting Bull comes down on the Union Pacific, the process of scalping will no doubt be considerably simplified in the case of these Celestials. The type of scalpee will appear to him to have reached its highest development. I suggest this as a solution of the Chinese problem where all will be satisfied, save, possibly, the Chinese.

H. C. C.

Daily Alta California, September 11, 1876

RED CLOUD AGENCY

Special to the Alta

Camp Robinson, Nebraska, Red Cloud Agency, September 1st, 1876.

The celerity with which the Fourth Artillery battalion proceeded from San Francisco to Cheyenne was compensated for in the universal law of nature by the lack of speed with which they proceeded from Cheyenne to this place. After lying at Cheyenne for two days, which were occupied in preparing for field service, it took up its line of march. Our preparations were simple, and consisted mainly in articles of food and clothing. Six days were consumed in crossing the ninety-three miles from Cheyenne to Fort Laramie. To the ordinary mind this seems long, but to ordinary legs it is not so, but, as the French say, "all contraire." Gentle lounging up and down Kearny street is not calculated to fit one for the business-like step required to cover one's three-miles-per-hour on the Laramie plains. Excoriated heels and excited bunions, not to mention blisters and irritated corns, were presented daily to the discriminating gaze of the attending surgeon. The fancy boots and well-fitting shoes, which personal pride prescribed in San Francisco, were relegated incontinently to the deepest recesses of valise or knapsack, and all resorted to the inelegant but comfortable "brass-screwed Jefferson rights and lefts," furnished by a paternal Government for the use of its soldiery. Fitted out in these and arrayed in our most disreputable garments, we looked as if returning from a long campaign, instead of entering upon one.

The dreary monotony of the plains cannot be appreciated until one has marched over them. As far as the eye reaches nothing could be seen but the dry, parched level. Rain has evidently been a rarity. The grasshoppers, however, accompanied us, as who should say "here is greenness." Every time a weary foot was advanced to plant itself fourteen inches nearer our point of destination, countless numbers of these cheerful insects arose into the hot air and buzzed away astonished. The only other signs of life were an occasional rattlesnake and a semi-occasional prairie dog or gopher. The reptiles did not manifest much aggressiveness, but rather sought to avoid us. Three or four, however, coiled themselves into attitudes of hostility, but the butt end of a musket or a ready sword crushed the incipient outbreak, and their rattles were added to the collection of trophies. The prairie dogs regarded us with curiosity, but on the vaguest suspicion of hostility vanished with contemptuous flirting of their diminutive tails into the recesses of their subterranean homes. One day we passed quite a colony of owls, who calmly viewed us with staring eyes, unsuspicious of danger. Attempts being made, however, to capture them, resulted in showing that their optical arrangements were equally calculated for day and night, and, although inelegant in their movements, they managed to preserve their liberty. On nearly the end of each day's journey a few rabbits and hares would be shot, which, made into stews, gave a variety to our menage both healthful and pleasant. Occasionally a courier or a party of miners would be met, and thus we passed along.

We remained two days at Fort Laramie, which is a post of some size and age. Then we cut loose from semblance of civilization—for a regular mail coach and telegraphic wires run to the post.

The Black Hills Stage Company runs a tri-weekly line of coaches from there to Cheyenne. This is coaching with a vengeance. Six to eight horses going at a jump, whirl the vehicle from Cheyenne to Laramie in one day, from sun up to sun down. Colonel De Lancey Kane would open his eyes if he saw this outfit.[19] The only spectators who usually gaze at it are the untutored savages, and as they glance along the barrel of a breech-loader, it requires nerve as well as skill to handle it. Each passenger assumes all risks, and, to the better provide against them, carries a small arsenal with him. The driver, besides the ordinary professional whip, is accoutered with a rifle and a good store of cartridges, and the journey is frequently enlivened by running fights.

We thought we had seen hard marching from Cheyenne to Laramie, but the four days we consumed reaching here proved the contrary. Marches have to be accommodated to the supply of wood and water in this country. The first day out we carried our wood, but marched twenty miles to water; the second was twenty-six miles; the third, sixteen; and the last twelve. We sighed for the cool afternoon breeze of San Francisco in vain.

On reaching the White River Springs we left the prairie and passed through the cañon through which the White River flows. It is very beautiful, free of trees and grass, and bordered by abrupt and romantic hills. As we debouched we met our first Indians, for we were now within a few miles of the Agency. The first specimen of the red man of the forest was a tall Arrapahoe [*sic*], lounging along, herding a lot of ponies. A few minutes walk and a large camp of this band appeared, nearly one hundred lodges. These lodges are principally of white cloth and shaped like the old Sibley tent. Groups of squaws made their appearance and probably discussed our appearance, as we did theirs. Youngsters, imperfect as to dress, ran out and gazed, but we kept along, passing other smaller camps until we reached Camp Robinson, beyond which, about two miles and within a mile of the Red Cloud Agency, we made the camp at which we are now, and from appearances are likely to remain. Orders have been issued to build winter quarters.

We have made our plans, and will probably be hard at work at them by the time this reaches you. The first two or three days have been consumed in settling down in our camp.

Night before last, however, we were ordered to be in readiness at 4 A.M. for possible hostilities. Gen. Mackenzie, the commanding officer, desired to arrest several bad Indians, and to prepare for trouble ordered the whole command under arms. The command here consists of six troops of the Fourth Cavalry, two of the Fifth, two companies of Fourteenth Infantry, our four of the Fourth Artillery, besides three companies of the Ninth Infantry, in the post proper, and one company of the Fifth Cavalry occupied in scouting and courier service—making in all eighteen companies, or about eight hundred men.

The First Cavalry battalion left camp early yesterday morning and marched to the Indian village to the northeast of the agency,[20] where they captured some of the Indians wanted. The rest of us stood at arms, interested spectators of this movement. From our position we could see the long line of troopers appear and disappear behind the hills, the galloping to and fro of orderlies and staff officers, the groups of interested Indians in adjacent camps, and all the pomp and panoply of prospective war. After about an hour's absence the column returned, but when within half a mile of camp they retraced their steps, again losing themselves behind the hills. Various were the surmises as to the reason of this, but we had to content ourselves with conjecture until from the distance was heard two shots. We waited with impatience further reports, but no more followed, and presently the cavalry returned and slowly marched to camp. All this took place in the grey of the morning, and to those of us who had not seen any hostile demonstrations for years, the recollections of the war came back afresh; and to those who never had seen any, the movements of this cavalry column, the heavy column in reserve, our own men standing in their company streets, with their equipments and one hundred rounds of ammunition, the mysterious movements of the troopers, the running to and fro of the Indians, all presented a scene rendered more vivid by the feeling that we ourselves would be starting out next.

Daylight arrived, and with it came the news that the shots heard were fired by one Indian, and killed another. The Indian killed rejoiced in the name of Sioux Jim, and was one of those General Mackenzie wanted. Being absent at the time, he returned after the cavalry left, and was incontinently shot by American Horse, who remarked that he didn't want Sioux Jim around the camp to bring any more incursions of the same nature upon it. The precision and promptitude with which the aforesaid American Horse acted is deserving of all praise. As one of our cavalry confreres remarked, there are now two good Indians the more—the one who shot and the one who was shot.[21] These movements over, the regular ten days' issue of rations took place at the Agency, and parties of bucks and squaws were going and returning all day. Their meat is issued on the hoof. This is undoubtedly to save the trouble of killing, but the Indians seize upon it to enact as near a representation of a buffalo hunt as possible with these tame villatic cattle. A grand blow-out usually accompanies ration-day, but as we were all held in camp, I am unable to give you a description. It is reserved for another issue.

It is impossible to tell how many Indians there are here. A great many are now like young gentlemen of fortune of the time of Queen Anne, "making the campaign" with Sitting Bull. They will probably return to their estates during the Winter. We learn that the Peace Commission is on the way; also that Crook and Terry's campaign is over for the year. You know all this better than we. As for news, this is the last place in the world to get it. A newspaper is as much of a rarity as snow in August. We don't know what new enormity the

Camp Canby, Nebraska, was a hovel of rough-hewn log and dirt-roofed structures located along the White River mid-way between Camp Robinson and Red Cloud Agency. *Larry Ness Collection*

Republicans are guilty of, nor how many times the bloody shirt has been shaken.

The health of the command is good, and its appetite is something abnormal. This is a fine place for eating.

H. C. C.

Daily Alta California, October 2, 1876

IN THE BLACK HILLS

Special to the Alta

Deadwood, Wyoming, September 20th.

Here is a faithful picture of the Commanding General of the Department of the Platte, as he emerged from the recesses of the Black Hills, and thrust upon the gaze of the assembled Fourth Artillery: Two days hard marching, over roads at which a Hank Monk would have moderated his fabled speed, had brought our supply train to the banks of the Box Elder, and within twenty-two miles of Deadwood, the mining town par excellence of the Black Hills. Our journey for the day was completed; the happy mules grazed leisurely along the river bottom, and the troops watched with subdued impatience the gradual preparation of their coffee; the officers were eating lunch, and the principal serenity of the camp seemed destined to continue, when the pickets in front announced the approach of a mounted party, from whom an avant courier shortly appeared, announcing that it was General Crook and escort en route to Camp Robinson. This news created an agreeable excitement—all rose to welcome the party, who shortly appeared—a quiet, middle-aged man, habited in a suit of gray citizen's clothes and riding a sedate and business-like white horse, who plodded along totally oblivious of his real rank among his equine comrades. The pantaloons of this General were stuffed irregularly in his boot legs, and his chapeau was a soft felt, of most modest and negligent appearance. The sandy, long beard appertaining to the Commanding General was ingeniously woven into two plaits, which, to say the least, gave him a very bizarre appearance. Across his saddle pommel lay a Springfield rifle and around his waist was strapped a prairie belt, plentifully garnished with central-fire metallic cartridges, caliber, 45, ready for any emergency, aboriginal or sylvan.

The countenance of this General was impressive, and he rode into our camp seemingly unconscious that he possessed the power to make us all "hump." This last is a very impressive word. I do not know whether it is "Worchester," or even "Webster," but it nevertheless is well known and conceals within its four component parts a variety of meanings, varying with its application. The Staff followed, generally arrayed in butternut shirts and overalls, a style of dress peculiarly affected by the denizens of these parts; while in the rear of them came the escort chastely decked with a fine assortment of patches. Interspersed among the foregoing were several correspondents of Eastern papers regarding each other with professional animosity and severally cogitating the character and composition of the item this incident suggested. In rear of all rode an imperturbable Ute Indian, the solitary representative of the race, while the extreme and final rear was composed of about 20 pack mules, who meandered through the adjacent thickets totally regardless of order and scornful of expostulation. To them a bell mule, mature and experienced, was law and prophet. At the tinkle of her bell they advanced or halted, and as her movements were controlled by one of

Brigadier General George Crook commanded the Department of the Platte, which included the Fourth Artillery during the Great Sioux War. *Library of Congress*

the superior race his jerking her to a standstill brought this asinine mob to a state of rest.

In the meantime, a new lunch being prepared, we fed the wayfarers, and learned from them the news, which you probably are already apprised of through the instrumentality of the ingenious invention of Professor Morse—in short, as Mr. Micawber would say—the telegraph. The campaign from its beginning has been an exceptionally severe one, and the appearance of this party proved it. The fight of two weeks ago at Slim Buttes has been the only one of any consequence since the Rosebud. The intervening time has been used up in unavailing efforts to bring the astute Sitting Bull to toe the scratch, in hard marches, hard living and general hardship, enlivened by the knowledge that those who know all about it, were wanting to know why the devil Crook didn't do something. We ourselves were gratified to know that we carried the first regular supplies to the little army, more especially as we are led to believe that we had exceeded the anticipations of the General in the speed of our march. One hundred and forty miles, with heavily loaded wagons, in a little over seven days through the Black Hills road, is doing pretty well. General Crook ordered us to unload where we were, and leaving Company K, Fourth Artillery, to guard the supplies until his own train came for them, to return to Red Cloud.

After giving this order he and his party started up, and the last we saw was a remorseless whip lash descend with vigor and precision on the dilatory hind-quarters of a vanishing pack mule.

Unloading on the afternoon of the 17th, we retraced our way and are now fifteen miles from Red Cloud.

The Black Hills country deserves some notice, especially in a letter to a paper published in a mining community. As a mining sharp, I don't profess to any pretensions. I am totally unable to talk intelligibly about "pay dirt," "bed rock," the showing of "color," or the assay to the ton of quartz. Custer City is the first mining locality we struck. They say—please note the indefiniteness of this—"they say" that there is good mining here, but they haven't got the water; that good quartz has been found, and that when the water comes and the streams are full that the claims will pay.

Passing Custer we struck, every few miles, small mining camps which had been deserted for the superior attractions of Deadwood. One melancholy miner said there was gold there, but no water. Hill City, an embryotic metropolis of about 140 log huts, has some good claims, "they say." Then comes Golden City, Rapid and Spring Creek, where they have water, but not much gold, and at last Deadwood.

We did not get to Deadwood, but we saw many parties hastening there. There is undoubtedly gold there, for one party had passed down with $400,000 worth of dust, while we heard of a party of colored gentlemen who had gotten out $600,000 worth from their claims, and were seeking to get to the States with it. These fortunate sons of Ham, it seems, are stampeded with their own success. They probably consider that they have no rights which white men or red men are bound to respect. Let us hope they will get through. With $600,000 worth of gold dust in their pockets, they will undoubtedly be permitted to ride in the most exclusive horse-car on the continent. Their less fortunate brothers of the paler countenance will be ejected from reserved seats in the orchestra chairs, in order that they may be accommodated under the provisions of the Fifteenth Amendment; and lastly, the most autocratic hotel clerk will find rooms, with baths, on the first floor for them; while the seats nearest to the Captain, at the first table on river steamers, will be turned down to await their coming. As Ancient Pistol has it, "I sing of Africa and golden joys," if only they can pass the dangers of Red Cañon or Buffalo Gap.[22]

Deadwood felicitates itself on being the wickedest city of the period. Marvelous tales are told of it, but how far true they are cannot be substantiated by your correspondent. The country between Custer and Deadwood is exceedingly wild and romantic. Some beautiful little valleys lie perdue in the mountains. Game is abundant off the main road, elk and deer being plentiful. We do not wonder that the Sioux objected to giving up the Black Hills, especially when we view the country round the Bad Lands. Let, however, no man go to the Black Hills without a good rifle and store of ammunition, for, as was remarked by a hardy miner to me, "The Injuns is making things lively. They scalp a man or two every day. I see two men they killed down about Custer. They was scalped—and d——n well scalped they was, too." Upon which this hardy miner slung his Winchester rifle over his saddle-bow, and departed to prospect in a locality peculiarly affected by the redmen aforesaid—and I experienced a renewed predilection for a paper currency.

H. C. C.

NOTES

1. William T. Sherman, "Report of the General of the Army," 10 Nov. 1876, in *Report of the Secretary of War, 1876* (Washington, D.C.: Government Printing Office, 1876), pp. 35 (quotations), 36.

2. Paul L. Hedren, *Great Sioux War Orders of Battle: How the United States Army Waged War on the Northern Plains, 1876–1877* (Norman, Okla.: Arthur H. Clark Co., 2011), pp. 59–65, 88, 189–208; "Reinforcements Going Forward," *Daily Alta California* (San Francisco), 16 Aug. 1876.

3. Fourth Artillery Regimental Returns, July, 1876, Microcopy 727, Roll 30, National Archives and Records Service, Washington, D.C.; Theo. F. Rodenbough and William L. Haskins, eds., *The Army of the United States* (1896; reprint ed., New York: Argonaut Press, 1966), pp. 372–73; Erwin N. Thompson, *Modoc War: Its Military History & Topography* (Sacramento, Calif.: Argus Books, 1971), p. 172.

4. Hedren, *Great Sioux War Orders of Battle*, pp. 88, 189–208; Thompson, *Modoc War*, pp. 173, 175; William J. Roe, "Walter Howe," in *Forty-Sixth Annual Reunion of the Association of the Graduates of the United States Military Academy, at West Point, New York, June 12th, 1916* (Saginaw, Mich.: Seemann and Peters, 1916), p. 95.

5. *Records of Living Officers of the United States Army* (Philadelphia: L. R. Hamersley and Co., 1884), pp. 39, 219; Francis B. Heitman, *Historical Register and Dictionary of the United States Army*, 2 vols. (1903; reprint ed., Urbana: University of Illinois Press, 1965), 1:347–48.

6. "The Indian War," *Daily Alta California*, 12 Aug. 1876.

7. Thomas R. Buecker, *Fort Robinson and the American West, 1874–1899* (Lincoln: Nebraska State Historical Society, 1999), p. 86; "Red Cloud Agency," *Daily Alta California*, 11 Sept. 1876.

8. John G. Bourke, *On the Border with Crook* (New York: Charles Scribner's Sons, 1891), p. 386; Charles M. Robinson III, *The Diaries of John Gregory Bourke, Volume 2, July 29, 1876–April 7, 1878* (Denton: University of North Texas Press, 2005), p. 140; "In the Black Hills," *Daily Alta California*, 2 Oct. 1876.

9. "In the Black Hills," *Daily Alta California*, 2 Oct. 1876; Charles King, *Campaigning with Crook and Stories of Army Life* (New York: Harper and Brothers, 1890), p. 147 (quotations).

10. Hedren, *Great Sioux War Orders of Battle*, pp. 141–47. The standard history of this campaign and battle is Jerome A. Greene, *Morning Star Dawn: The Powder River Expedition and the Northern Cheyennes, 1876* (Norman: University of Oklahoma Press, 2003).

11. *Daily Alta California*, 14 Jan. 1877 (first quotation); "Personal Paragraphs," *Omaha Daily Bee*, 11 Jan. 1877 (second quotation); J. P. Sanger, "Joseph B. Campbell," in *Twenty-Third Annual Reunion of the Association of the Graduates of the*

United States Military Academy, at West Point, New York, June 9th, 1892 (Saginaw, Mich.: Seemann and Peters, 1892), p. 20 (third quotation).

12. William J. Roe, "Walter Howe," in *Forty-Sixth Annual Reunion of the Association of the Graduates of the United States Military Academy*, pp. 96–97.

13. "George G. Greenough," in *Forty-Fourth Annual Reunion of the Association of the Graduates of the United States Military Academy, at West Point, New York, June 11th, 1913* (Saginaw, Mich.: Seemann and Peters, 1913), p. 45; "Gen. G. G. Greenough Dies," *New York Times*, 28 June 1912; "Gen. Franklin 'Frank' Guest Smith," in *American Biographical Directories: District of Columbia* (Washington, D.C.: Potomac Press, 1908), p. 434; "Gen Franklin 'Guest' Smith," www.findagrave.com.

14. Sanger, "Joseph B. Campbell," pp. 17–22.

15. Wirt Robinson, ed., *Biographical Register of the Officers and Graduates of the United States Military Academy at West Point, New York* (Saginaw, Mich.: Seemann and Peters, 1920), p. 182.

16. Terrace, Utah, was a landmark community on the Central Pacific Railroad located west of the Great Salt Lake midway between Ogden and the Nevada line. Richard V. Francaviglia, *Over the Range: A History of the Promontory Summit Route of the Pacific Railroad* (Logan: Utah State University Press, 2008), pp. 178–80.

17. This is a reference to Crook's small but newsworthy fight with the Sioux in the Slim Buttes. For particulars, *see* Jerome A. Greene, *Slim Buttes, 1876: An Episode of the Great Sioux War* (Norman: University of Oklahoma Press, 1982); and Paul L. Hedren, ed., *Ho! For the Black Hills: Captain Jack Crawford Reports the Black Hills Gold Rush and Great Sioux War* (Pierre: South Dakota Historical Society Press, 2012), chaps. 7 and 8.

18. John Ruskin was a widely published English art critic, social thinker, and philanthropist. Among his books readily available in America during Cushing's time were *The Crown of Wild Olive: Three Lectures on Work, Traffic and War* (1866) and *Fors Clavigera: Letters to the Workmen and Labourers of Great Britain* (1871).

19. Cushing refers to the horse-drawn "Pelham Coach" driven by Colonel Delancey Kane that traveled the boroughs of New York City. The story of Kane and this coach inspired three popular songs published in 1876. Blake A. Bell, "Col. Delancey Kane and 'The Pelham Coach,'" *Pelham* (N.Y.) *Weekly*, 26 Sept. 2003.

20. The reference is to an assembly of cavalry present for duty at Camp Robinson, not a literal First Cavalry Regiment.

21. William Garnett, a mixed-blood interpreter and stalwart figure at Camp Robinson and Red Cloud Agency, remembered Sioux Jim as a tough character, a thief and robber without honor. A member of the Loafer Band, Sioux Jim was the brother of Little Big Man. Richard E. Jensen, *The Indian Interviews of Eli S. Ricker, 1903–1919*, Voices of the American West, volume 1 (Lincoln: University of Nebraska

Press, 2005), p. 96; Thomas Powers, *The Killing of Crazy Horse* (New York: Alfred A. Knopf, 2010), p. 219.

22. Red Cañon and Buffalo Gap were critical entryways into the Black Hills on the Cheyenne and Sidney roads, respectively. Both were extremely narrow defiles notoriously plagued by Indians and road agents.

3 : **Shoot Today and Kill Tomorrow** The Function and Evolution of Artillery during the Indian Campaigns, 1866–1890

DOUGLAS C. MCCHRISTIAN

The nature of Indian warfare on the western frontier dictated that cavalry, supported in many instances by infantry, played the dominant role in active campaigning. However, artillery, operating as units in their intended tactical role, was rarely evident. During the post–Civil War era the five artillery regiments authorized for the Regular Army were stationed primarily along the nation's eastern and southern seacoasts, usually manning large masonry fortifications strategically placed to defend important cities and harbors from enemy invasion. The single exception was the Second Artillery, posted initially on the Pacific Coast to man forts in the vicinity of San Francisco Bay and to guard the mouth of the strategic Columbia River. Following United States acquisition of Alaska in 1867, the army transferred some of its companies to that far-off territory to protect American interests.[1]

At the outset of the Civil War, all regular artillery companies, the only trained and experienced units then available, were redesignated as "light" or field batteries. Horse-drawn light artillery was urgently needed to support infantry in field operations, whereas newly organized volunteer artillery units were largely marshaled in the defenses surrounding Washington, D.C., where they could be trained at a somewhat more leisurely pace.

The regular "red legs," nicknamed for the color of their trouser stripes, served as light artillery for the duration of the war. An 1865 general order, however, directed that only two companies or "batteries" of each regiment were thereafter to remain mounted. The others reverted to foot or heavy units performing garrison duty and manning large-bore guns in the coastal defenses. Colonels were granted discretion to designate which two companies of their respective regiments were to be the light batteries. The order further stipulated that one of the light batteries was to be armed with four 12-pounder smooth-bore field guns, the other with four wrought-iron 3-inch rifles, both of which had proven to be the mainstays of the federal artillery. Members of light batteries rode either on horseback or aboard the limbers and caissons to maximize mobility.[2]

Following the postwar reorganization of the field artillery, however, no one in the army was quite sure what to do with it. While most of those units remained at stations on or near the sea coasts, three mounted batteries were sent to the western plains in 1866: Battery C, Third Artillery, to the Department of the Platte; Battery B of the Fifth to the Department of the Arkansas; and one battery of the Fourth Artillery to the Department of the Missouri at Fort Leavenworth, Kansas. Presumably, they were to be available for potential service in the regions currently experiencing increased Indian trouble.[3]

To counter depredations arising across western Kansas the next year, Major General Winfield S. Hancock, commanding the Department of the Missouri, organized a sizable expedition at Fort Leavenworth. His mission was either to coerce the marauders to accept peace terms or to defeat them in battle. Augmenting a force composed of several companies of the Seventh Cavalry and Thirty-Seventh Infantry, the Fourth's Light Battery B joined the expedition to add the muscle of its four guns. Hancock, an inexperienced Indian fighter fresh from major combat commands during the war, failed to realize the futility of trying to bring artillery to bear against fleet mounted warriors.

Hancock's force, totaling some 1,400 men, marched southwest via Forts Harker and Larned before striking west up Pawnee Creek in search of a combined Cheyenne and Oglala Lakota village. When at length the camp was located on an open plain, Hancock arrayed his force in an impressive line of battle, infantry on the left, artillery in the center, cavalry on the right. Nevertheless, a fight failed to materialize after the headmen parleyed with Hancock long enough to allow the rest of the villagers to escape during the night, leaving the army holding an empty bag. Electing not to follow the Indian trail with his ponderous column, the general directed Lieutenant Colonel George A. Custer and his cavalry to pursue the Indians northward, while the balance of the expedition made a circuitous march south to Fort Dodge, then north to Fort Hays. There Hancock detached Battery B, ordering it to return to its home station without having fired a shot in anger. Thus, what might have been an unparalleled opportunity to bring an entire battery of regular field artillery to bear against Indians on the plains came to naught.[4]

A few months later Captain Albert Barnitz, Seventh Cavalry, observed the battery formed for its eastward march from Fort Harker and was profoundly impressed with a sight rarely seen on the frontier: "This morning Capt. Parson's Light Battery 'B,' 4th Artillery left this Post for Fort Leavenworth. . . . It presented a fine appearance, as it moved out,—6 [*sic*] pieces of Artillery, each drawn by 6 horses, 6 caissons and limber-boxes, and two forges, each drawn by 6 horses, and cannoneers all mounted, and 22 wagons. . . . The Artillery drill is quite imposing."[5]

An 1869 congressional cost-cutting act further pared the size of the army by eliminating one light battery from each regiment. Mounted units with their horses and equipment were more expensive to maintain than foot companies, so the army retained only five light batteries.

That spring four of those batteries took station at Fort Riley, Kansas, where the army determined to establish a light artillery school.[6] The barren Great Plains presented a stark contrast to the artillerymen, most of whom had spent their lives east of the Mississippi River. Soon after arriving at the post, one soldier sarcastically recorded his impression: "Westward lies the valley through which run the Kansas and Republican Rivers, neither larger than a good-sized New England brook; and the little town of Junction City, happy in its dirt, its enterprise, and its obscurity, is part of the view. The fort . . . is said to be the pet post of the Plains. Its quarters are admirable, its stables excellent, and its drill ground extends over hundreds of miles."[7]

Further Indian trouble in western Kansas unexpectedly forestalled the army's plan for a central training facility. A triple-pronged campaign against the southern plains tribes in the Texas Panhandle and western Indian Territory during the winter of 1868–69, while strategically successful, had the effect of driving some of the hostile bands far northward. Consequently, spring witnessed renewed Indian raids along the route of the Kansas Pacific Railroad and against settlers residing in the valleys of the Smoky Hill, Republican, and Solomon Rivers. The available cavalry was already overextended, so the department commander dispatched two of the light batteries at Fort Riley (K, First and A, Second Artillery) to the field in June on an expedition against marauding Cheyennes. In this instance, the red legs were armed, equipped, and mounted as cavalry. The two companies remained on the plains most of the summer, patrolling north-central and northwest Kansas. In their one brief encounter with hostiles, the artillerymen successfully repulsed warriors who attacked the column's flankers. Once the Indian threat was thwarted, the command returned to Fort Riley in mid-August.[8]

In spring 1870, Indian forays resumed along travel routes and settled areas throughout western Kansas, southwestern Nebraska, and eastern Colorado Territory. The light artillerymen at Fort Riley again were pressed into service as makeshift cavalry to aid in quelling the raiding. An expedition composed of 228 officers and men of the Second, Third, and Fourth Artillery took the field in June to patrol the region west of the post and north of the line of the Kansas Pacific Railroad connecting Kansas City with Denver. The column remained out until September, without encountering any of the illusive warriors yet providing an essential military presence in the region.[9]

The four light batteries continued to garrison Fort Riley for the next six months, when elements of the Sixth Cavalry arrived to relieve them. During April and May 1871, the units were ordered to rejoin their respective regiments at stations in the East, except for A Battery, Second Artillery, which returned to its former home in California.[10]

Until the mid-1870s, virtually all field and mountain guns found on the frontier dated to the Civil War or earlier. The Model 1841 12-pounder mountain howitzer was particularly popular early on, because of its small size and portability. The piece, complete with carriage, weighed a total of only 575 pounds. The so-called prairie carriage, with a wider wheelbase than the original mountain pattern, could traverse uneven terrain with little danger of tipping over. A team of only two horses or mules was required to pull both the ammunition cart, known as a limber, and the attached howitzer. When circumstances required, however, the piece could be easily broken down into three major components (tube, carriage, and wheels) and transported almost anywhere on the backs of two mules, with a ready supply of ammunition carried on a third animal.[11]

The howitzer, with a bore diameter of 4.62 inches, was capable of firing three types of projectiles: explosive shell and spherical case shot, both of which were fused, and canister. (Solid shot was not used in the mountain howitzer.) The tube was cast with a chamber of smaller diameter suited for a tapered cartridge containing an 8-ounce charge of black cannon powder. Firing an explosive shell weighing only 9.35 pounds, the short-barreled howitzer could lob the ball to a maximum range of about 1,005 yards. Shell, designed for use against nonmasonry structures and for counterbattery fire, was not particularly effective against dispersed footmen because relatively few pieces of shrapnel resulted from the shattered cast iron ball. More effective was spherical case shot containing eighty-two .69-caliber lead balls surrounding a small bursting charge. Weighing some three pounds more than a shell, spherical case had a limited range to only about 800 yards under ideal conditions. The third type of ammunition, canister, consisted of a thin sheet-iron can containing 148 .69-caliber lead balls packed in sawdust. The projectile weighed slightly more than eleven pounds and was fired point-blank, similar to a shotgun, at enemy concentrations at ranges up to about two hundred yards. All ammunition was fixed: the projectile was strapped with strips of tin to the top of a wood sabot and a woolen powder bag was tacked to the bottom edge. This formed a complete cartridge that was easily handled and loaded into the tube.[12]

The friction primer, a small brass tube filled with fulminate, was used for discharging all types of muzzle-loading pieces of the era. After the charge was rammed home, one crew member inserted a pointed rod called a priming wire into the vertical vent at the breach to perforate the powder bag. With the charge thus exposed, a soldier standing opposite placed the primer in the vent and hooked the lanyard through the wire loop of the rubber (striker). Stepping to one side at the length of the lanyard, he pulled it at right angles to discharge the piece at the gunner's command "fire."[13]

Many posts used the diminutive bronze howitzers only as salute guns, but the neighboring garrisons of Fort Phil Kearny, Dakota Territory, and Fort C. F. Smith, Montana Territory, in the heart of the contested lands claimed by the Sioux and Northern Cheyennes, made more frequent combat use of the howitzer than perhaps any other western stations. Just a few months after the army occupied the Bozeman Trail, Lieutenant Colonel William J. Fetterman led an eighty-man battalion out of Fort Phil Kearny and was ambushed and overwhelmed by hundreds of warriors concealed in ravines on either side of the road. Just as the fight ended, a relief party armed with a howitzer topped the ridge above the battle site. Quickly unlimbering the gun to drive off the warriors, an infantry corporal recounted that "I was one of the detachment to handle the artillery and we certainly shelled those Indians."[14] They were nevertheless too late to save anyone of Fetterman's command.

The little howitzers indeed proved their worth in dispersing enemy concentrations on several occasions. War parties hovered near both of the beleaguered Bozeman Trail posts in anticipation of ambushing small or unwary groups of soldiers venturing beyond the stockades. First Lieutenant George M. Templeton, a Twenty-Seventh Infantry officer at Fort C. F. Smith, recorded an incident in April 1867 in which a mountain howitzer helped to save a detachment of soldiers. "Indians to the number of 30 or more again tried to capture [a] patrol. H & D Co[mpanie]s rushed out and with the mounted party followed three miles. Took one howitzer and fired two shells at them." An Eighteenth Infantryman, Corporal Alexander Brown, commented that at Fort Phil Kearny "me and two of the boys had a cannon on the parade ground. We used to go and shell them [Indians] to keep them away from the stockade." A mountain howitzer from Fort Phil Kearny also helped to end one of the most famous engagements in frontier history, the Wagon Box Fight of August 1867. Surmounting a nearby hill, a rescuing party from the garrison effectively used a howitzer to break up a large number of Sioux assembling for another assault on the surrounded soldiers. One of the men inside the corral of dismounted wagon boxes, Private Samuel Gibson, observed the effect: "We . . . sat watching the skirmish line advancing, while the boom of the big gun was the sweetest sound that ever fell on our ears. The gunners were throwing shells into a big bunch of Indians in the

Big Piney valley." Sergeant Max Littman remembered that one of the shells "exploded very close to where the main body of savages were congregated. At this shot the Indians fled from the field."[15]

The portability of the stubby mountain howitzer, with a tube barely thirty-three inches long, was offset by its limited range. It was further handicapped by being a smoothbore and thus was capable of only indifferent accuracy at extreme ranges. For example, when the soldiers of a detachment approaching Fort Casper, Wyoming Territory, were fired upon by a howitzer crew that mistook them for Indians, Private William F. Hynes (alias William Jones) scoffed, "The shell fell short, but made an awful fuss in scattering sand and dirt. We knew the limitations of that battery and did not fear it."[16]

Such experiences caused many frontier commanders to conclude that the mountain howitzer lacked the range and accuracy necessary for plains warfare. The Model 1857 light 12-pounder gun, nicknamed the "Napoleon" for its French origin, was much larger and heavier than its little cousin. In contradiction to its nomenclature, gun and carriage weighed nearly 3,500 pounds, making the Napoleon cumbersome to transport over broken, trackless terrain and too slow to get into action for most Indian engagements. Despite those disadvantages, the Napoleon could throw a shell some 1,300 yards or case shot over 1,100 yards, with a fair degree of accuracy. Canister for the Napoleon contained 27 large iron balls that could be devastating to personnel at ranges up to 400 yards. Its rapidity of fire when manned by trained crews was often the deciding factor in the conventional battles of the Civil War.[17]

Artillery pieces with rifled bores exerting a football-like spin to elongated projectiles were just making their debut at the beginning of the Civil War. Perhaps the best of those was the gracefully executed 3-inch ordnance rifle introduced in 1861 and produced in large quantities throughout the war. Through a process patented by the Phoenix Iron Company in Pennsylvania, the tube was formed of wrought-iron bars wrapped and welded around a mandrel, machined to exterior and interior dimensions, and rifled with seven lands and grooves. This resulted in a tube that was not only stronger but considerably lighter than bronze guns. The tube itself tipped the scale at only 820 pounds, compared with the Napoleon's 1,227 pounds. Moreover, the lighter iron gun could be mounted on the same carriage used for the old Model 1841 six-pounder, weighing over 200 pounds less than the Napoleon carriage. Although somewhat slower to load, rifled guns possessed longer range and greater accuracy than smoothbores using round shot. The ordnance rifle, sometimes erroneously called a "Rodman" gun, could hurl an explosive 9-pound shell up to 1,830 yards with considerable accuracy. During the war, for example, a Confederate artilleryman grudgingly attested that "the Yankee three-inch rifle was a dead shot at any distance under a mile. They could hit the end of a flour barrel more often than miss, unless the gunner got excited." He went on to say that he witnessed the crew of a Union ordnance rifle place three successive shots through a fortress embrasure measuring only a foot wide. These factors were obvious reasons for the rifle's popularity for frontier service.[18]

Even though artillery units may have been a rarity in frontier service, various types of cannon were common at posts throughout the West. With few exceptions, every permanent military station had at least one gun for firing daily and special salutes with blank cartridges. Many boasted three to five pieces, not counting Gatling guns, which were classed not as artillery but rather as machine guns because of their comparatively small calibers and rapid fire. An 1876 tabulation of artillery pieces at posts in four western departments within the Division of the Missouri (Dakota, the Platte, the Missouri, and Texas) provides a useful perspective, particularly because that year generally represents the high-water mark of Indian conflict. Inventoried in these departments were 77 mountain howitzers, 40 light 12-pounder guns, 32 3-inch ordnance rifles, and 26 Model 1841 6-pounder guns (which were entirely obsolete by that time and were probably being used only for salute purposes and training). More heavily armed than most posts, Fort Laramie, Wyoming Territory, boasted a 12-pounder mountain howitzer, a 3-inch ordnance rifle, and four Napoleons.[19]

Indians were at once astonished and rightfully intimidated by artillery. In those rare instances when guns could be used against concentrated bodies of warriors, cannons proved to have a fearsome psychological effect. "They [Lakota Sioux] have a superstitious dread of artillery," opined Second Lieutenant Jonathan W. Biddle, Seventh Cavalry. Besides the sharp thunderous crack of a field piece, the secondary explosion and destructive force of an explosive projectile at a great distance from the gun were beyond the comprehension of most Indians. "Big guns heap bad," one Lakota Sioux chief grumbled to an interpreter. "They shoot today and kill tomorrow." Experienced warriors quickly learned to avoid whenever possible the wagon guns that "shot twice," as some Indians characterized them. The commanding officer at Fort Stevenson, Dakota Territory, recorded that he had two 3-inch rifles that he had seen used only once. "Two conical shells were enough to disperse a band of two or three hundred Indians who had announced their presence . . . by stealing four mules and killing a wagoner," he wrote. "One of them had his leg shot off by the first cannon shot, another was seriously wounded, and one of their horses was ripped open from a distance of 1800 yards where they thought they were out of firing range. They had enough and ran away on the gallop."[20]

In the absence of genuine artillerymen at frontier stations, infantry and cavalry soldiers commonly served as ad hoc gun crews. When needs arose, officers wisely took advantage of any former artillerymen who might be in their companies. A recurring occasion for cannon firing was Independence Day, when post commanders were required by regulations to fire a national salute at noon according to the number of states currently in the Union. "The 4th of July will soon be here, and from all appearances will be a dull one at this Post," Private Eddie Matthews wrote from Fort Union, New Mexico Territory. "There will be a National Salute of 37 Guns fired here. Have been drilling men here that are to fire the salute. They are men that have been in the . . . 'Artilery' [*sic*] before." A knowledgeable officer, frequently a West Pointer or a noncom with prior artillery service, was detailed as drill master.[21]

Serving an artillery piece was serious business that required strict adherence to the procedures laid down in the tactics manual. Every crew member had specific duties to perform in precise sequence in coordination with the other men. Mistakes could result in serious injury or death to a comrade. The most dangerous position was Number One, the man who sponged the bore after each shot to extinguish sparks then rammed home the next charge. Colonel Philippe Régis de Trobriand, Thirteenth Infantry, somberly described the horrific effect of a premature discharge during a July Fourth observance:

> The holiday was clouded and saddened by a serious accident. One of the gunners who served the pieces which were firing the salute had his right arm shot off by the premature discharge of the cannon into which he was ramming the charge. Of course the accident happened through the fault of number three who had the responsibility of sealing the vent hermetically and who let air get in through negligence or distraction. His [the victim's] name is Ch[arles] Ray [*sic*: Rhey]. During the war, he served in the artillery. It is a real tragedy to have come through deadly battles only to be mutilated while firing a peaceful salute.[22]

Number Three, standing to the right of the breech, wore a leather pad on this left thumb and was responsible for pressing it firmly over the vent to prevent any air from being drawn into the tube during sponging. As the sponge was withdrawn, air sucked into the bore could kindle a smoldering particle of powder bag from the previous shot. Then, as Number One rammed home the next charge, the glowing ember could cause a premature discharge at the very moment he firmly gripped the rammer shaft, costing him his right forearm.

Soldiers assigned to artillery duty also suffered injuries of a less serious nature. While serving on a gun crew firing a national salute in honor of Washington's Birthday at Fort Kearny, Nebraska, in February 1868, Sergeant Lauren W. Aldrich complained that he "was made deaf in my left ear by the firing . . . with a brass cannon." He failed to mention whether his injury was temporary or resulted in permanent hearing loss, but he nevertheless completed his enlistment.[23]

When artillery pieces accompanied troops in the field, as they often did on major expeditions, improvised gun crews were the norm. During the 1876 Sioux Campaign, for example, one soldier recalled that the heavy armament with Brigadier General Alfred H. Terry's Dakota Column included a 12-pounder Napoleon, an ordnance rifle, and two Gatling guns. "The drivers were cavalrymen," he noted, "and the cannoneers were a detachment of the 20th Infantry." It only made sense to place troopers, accustomed to caring for horses, in charge of the teams.[24]

Even though artillery rarely played a significant role in pitched combat with Indians, there were some noteworthy exceptions. The Fourth Artillery, transferred to stations on the West Coast in 1872, responded to Indian trouble the following year when the Modocs rose against white interlopers in northern California. After peace talks collapsed with the murder of Brigadier General Edward R. S. Canby, the army faced a unique challenge when the rebellious tribesmen took refuge in a rugged, nearly inaccessible area known as the Lava Beds. After infantry and dismounted cavalry failed to dislodge the warriors from their rocky bastions, even with the aid of a couple of mountain howitzers sent from Fort Vancouver, six batteries of the Fourth marched from their coastal stations to augment the troops already in the field. Four of those companies served as infantry and one (Light Battery B) as cavalry mounted on battery horses. However, one section of Battery A was armed with two mountain howitzers and another section with four Model 1841 24-pounder Coehorn mortars brought out of storage for this special circumstance. In the hands of capable artillerists, the mortars could lob 17-pound explosive shells into enemy positions at ranges up to 1,200 yards. However, in this instance, the crews probably had undergone little or no training with the old mortars. First Cavalryman Maurice Fitzgerald witnessed the opening shot:

> This baby mortar, intended for throwing shells into the stronghold just before an assault was made, arrived safely at our command. . . . The position taken was immediately behind Troop K, and we were to lie prone while it was being fired. It was loaded, sighted, and touched off, but through some oversight or defect, the shell, instead of being hurled behind the breastworks, fell about fifteen feet in front of our line and spun around, hissing and sputtering. . . . Some of the men jumped up and started to run; others seemed too dazed to move. An officer had the presence of mind to yell for everyone to hit the dirt just before the shell exploded, scattering fragments all around, but no one was injured.

The Battle of the Lava Beds proved to be the Fourth Artillery's most significant action during the era, at a cost of four officers and thirty-two men killed and wounded, most of them lost during a Modoc ambush of a battery serving as infantry.[25]

When Colonel David S. Stanley mounted an expedition accompanying Northern Pacific Railroad surveyors up Montana's Yellowstone

River in 1873, he took along a pair of ordnance rifles. The guns proved their value on 11 August near the end of an engagement between the Seventh Cavalry and a large number of Lakota warriors at the mouth of Allen Creek. First Lieutenant James C. Calhoun, Seventh Cavalry, commented: "On our way down to camp after fighting all day, we stopped to see the fireworks of Stanley shelling the Indians across the river. It was one of the prettiest sights I ever saw . . . Stanley shelled them . . . until they disappeared." It should be noted, however, that Stanley's ability to bring artillery into action under such circumstances was the exception.[26]

Throughout the remainder of the 1870s virtually no regular artillery served in its conventional role in the field. However, on several occasions artillery units reinforced troops on campaign or were temporarily assigned to backfill frontier garrisons during the absence of the cavalry and infantry. Three batteries of the Second Artillery, for example, were detailed from the East Coast to take station temporarily at Fort Dodge, Kansas, and posts in Indian Territory to replace garrisons called up for field service during 1876. In another instance, a four-company battalion of the Fourth, serving as infantry, participated in the Sioux War on the northern Great Plains during the fall and early winter of that year. In the 1878 campaign against the Bannocks, nine of the regiment's batteries took the field, one of them serving as cavalry and two as mounted infantry. Logically, those duties fell most frequently to the Fourth Artillery, stationed in the vicinity of the Presidio of San Francisco. From that point railroads rapidly transported the artillerymen to wherever they might be needed in the interior regions west of the Mississippi.[27]

Some field commanders chose to employ Napoleon guns, either by preference based on wartime experience or simply because they happened to be available at the base of operations. When three heavy expeditions of troops converged against the nontreaty Lakota Sioux and Northern Cheyennes in southeastern Montana Territory in spring 1876, Colonel John Gibbon's force, launched from Fort Ellis eastward down the Yellowstone River, was augmented by a light 12-pounder gun and two .50-caliber Gatling guns.[28] Large field pieces dictated to some extent a column's route of march and not infrequently posed a serious impediment. One of the soldiers in Gibbon's command, Second Cavalryman William F. Zimmer, pointed out the principal reason why many commanders declined to take cannons into the field: "The country . . . was very hilly & full of steep ravines, which gave us lots of trouble to take our 12 lb. Rodman [*sic*] Gun along, which was drawn by 8 horses. Sometimes [the] horses were unhitched and a whole co[mpany] would be pulling on a drag rope to get her up where the horses could get footing again."[29] The marginal value of field artillery in Indian fighting usually failed to compensate for the difficulty and frustration in moving field artillery across long distances in trackless frontier regions.

The Napoleon nevertheless came into play later that summer when Major Orlando H. Moore, commanding a battalion of the Sixth and Seventeenth Infantry, took his command down the Yellowstone River aboard a steamer to retrieve a quantity of forage left at an old supply depot. While the soldiers were resacking a huge pile of oats and conveying the grain aboard the boat, Sioux warriors began congregating in nearby gullies. Moore immediately deployed his men and positioned the 12-pounder and a Gatling gun to resist an attack. He wrote: "I then concluded to treat them with something new, and accordingly placed Lieutenant Woodruff's artillery in position, and opened fire upon a party on our right . . . with spherical case shell from our 12-pounder Napoleon gun, which spread consternation among them, and they were driven along from the ravine and fled to the bluff, as the shells went on their exploring expeditions, bearing more to the left [with?] each successive shot until the whole ground . . . on our left was commanded by our artillery."[30] Artillery proved its worth in this instance by dispersing the warriors before they were near enough to attack.

A few months later, following Lieutenant Colonel George A. Custer's defeat at the Battle of the Little Bighorn, the Sioux Expedition returned from the field and was concentrated at Fort Abraham Lincoln, Dakota Territory. According to an officer who was writing to his mother, the force included the reconstituted Seventh Cavalry, composed of "1100 fighting men (the whole regiment), two companies of the 6th Footpads [infantry], and a half battery of 3 inch rifle cannon manned by detailing men from the different companies who have served in the artillery. . . . They [Indians] have a superstitious dread of artillery, so if we can take their village, you will probably hear of the end of the Sioux war."[31] In the last act of the 1876 campaign season, the expedition proceeded down the Missouri River in late October to dismount and disarm the Sioux residing at the Standing Rock and Cheyenne River agencies. The artillery pieces, manned by men of the Twentieth Infantry, proved to be a significant factor in overawing the warriors into peaceful compliance.

Meanwhile, Division of the Missouri commander Lieutenant General Philip H. Sheridan had directed Colonel Nelson A. Miles and his Fifth Infantry to winter on the Yellowstone and establish a cantonment at the mouth of Tongue River in the heart of Sioux country. In October, while the troops were constructing the post, Miles received word that Sitting Bull's Lakotas had left the river county and were trekking northeast over the divide separating the watersheds of the Yellowstone and the Missouri Rivers. Intending to intercept the band before they could reach the assistance of their brethren at Fort Peck Agency, Miles ordered his entire regiment into the field. He wisely took along an ordnance rifle manned by some of his doughboys.

On 20 October, a few miles east of Cedar Creek, several hundred Sioux warriors arrayed along ridge tops confronted Miles's column. Indian messengers informed Miles that Sitting Bull wished to talk. Meeting between the lines, Miles and his principal officers engaged in protracted negotiations with the Lakota headmen but failed to arrive at any accord.[32]

Shortly after dawn on 21 October, Miles's infantry, deployed in extended battle formation, advanced up Cedar Creek. When they came within sight of the camp, the troops observed hundreds of villagers, principally the women, children, and elders, fleeing northward. Again warriors bearing a white flag and making peaceful overtures advanced toward the troops. Taking no chance of treachery, Miles posted one company on a commanding eminence and directed the officer commanding the ordnance rifle to position his gun on an adjacent high knoll.

At length Sitting Bull and other headmen arrived to talk with Miles. Although some of the chiefs indicated a willingness to surrender, Sitting Bull stubbornly insisted that he and his people be permitted to reside near and trade at Fort Peck. Miles just as adamantly refused to budge from his stance that the Sioux must surrender and move to Cantonment on Tongue River.

Miles concluded that an engagement was inevitable in order to break the stalemate. Early that afternoon he ordered his companies to advance toward the Indian positions on high ground several miles away. The entire line pressed forward, supported by the artillery, now repositioned on a flanking hill. Field Musician Edwin M. Brown, bugler for B Company, described the effect of the gun when it opened fire on the warriors about a mile away: "As we were down in the ravine the 'big gun' which was planted on the summit of a high bluff broke loose which scattered them [the Indians] in all directions; they kept so far away after the cannon opened on them that it was only our best marksmen were able to cause them to bite the dust."[33]

Choked by smoke from grass set afire by the warriors, the soldiers surged forward, sweeping the Sioux from the high ridges in front. Once over the crests, the troops descended on the village nestled below along Cedar Creek. Light skirmishing continued until dusk, when the troops pulled back to bivouac atop a high ridge.

The next day the Sioux took a southeasterly course, firing the prairie behind them and fighting rear-guard actions whenever the troops pressed too closely. Upon reaching the Yellowstone after a chase of twenty-seven miles, Miles discovered that the Indians had already crossed to the south side and made camp. The troops remained on the opposite bank with the intention of fording the river in the morning.

The ordnance rifle came into play a final time when a few warriors returned to the north bank and attempted to cut off the wagon master, who had left the column alone to bring up some straggling horses. Whipping his mule into a dead run, he managed to keep a safe distance from the pursuing Indians until mounted infantrymen and scouts rushed out to rescue him. "The men on the artillery wheeled the gun around," Brown declared, "and fired a shell among the Indians with such precision that it bursted immediately beneath the horses of the Indians; blankets, saddles, horses, riders and everything were seen flying in all directions." Unsurprisingly, the warriors peremptorily retreated.[34]

Miles subsequently met with Lakota leaders and learned that Sitting Bull and a hundred or more of his followers had left the main body to continue north toward the Missouri River to find buffalo. Offering to supply the remaining people with government rations, Miles induced the chiefs present to surrender and proceed to the agency on Cheyenne River. Catching Sitting Bull would have to wait.

Never idle for long, Miles saw another opportunity to strike hostile bands still in the Yellowstone country when they were at their weakest. He fully appreciated that the lack of forage for ponies would immobilize the warriors, thus presenting his doughboys with at least even odds of success. In January 1877, he led a battalion of his own Fifth Infantry, augmented by two companies of the Twenty-Second, up the valley of Tongue River seeking Crazy Horse's band of Oglala Sioux. With the Lakotas were a large number of Northern Cheyenne refugees from the village that Colonel Ranald S. Mackenzie's column had struck in the Big Horn Mountains the previous November. Hoping to catch the Indians hunkered down in their camps, Miles bolstered his force with a 3-inch rifle and a Napoleon gun teamed upstream from his rude cantonment. During the resulting Battle of Wolf Mountains, Miles's artillery section proved to be advantageous in dislodging warriors from their ridge top positions along the valley.[35]

Miles had long advocated using artillery in support of infantry to compensate for the cavalry's speed and mobility in breaking up warrior concentrations. As a soldier put it, "Indians could not stand the artillery fire."[36] Miles nevertheless considered the obsolete mountain howitzer too limited in range to be of much use against Indians in open country. Moreover, the field artillery available at the time offered a less than satisfactory alternative. "The chief objections to our Field Guns is their great weight," Miles rightly observed, "and to the Gatling Guns their weight and small calibre. I have used both in Indian fights, and it is impossible to determine the range of the latter at twelve or fifteen hundred yards."[37] His point was that bullets of .45 or .50 caliber were not large enough to produce a visible impact at long range, so it was nearly impossible to make the corrections necessary to strike the intended target.

Miles outlined the criteria for what he considered to be an appropriate field piece for Indian fighting. His principal consideration was weight, which he thought should not exceed 500 pounds for both tube and carriage. He further recommended that such a piece should be "a rifled gun, probably a breech-loader, that can travel with cavalry, and has an effective shell range beyond that of rifled small-arms, not less than 1,500 yards."[38]

Rifle guns at Pine Ridge Agency. Photograph by W. R. Cross, Hot Springs, S.Dak., 1891. *South Dakota State Historical Society*

Miles may have been unaware that a gun exceeding his vision already existed. Only recently, American arms inventor Benjamin B. Hotchkiss had designed a diminutive 1.65-inch (42 mm) breechloading rifle with a total weight of only 336 pounds. The gun was chambered for a brass-cased cartridge containing a 6-ounce powder charge and a 2-pound nose-detonated explosive shell containing shrapnel. Having an effective range of up to about 2,000 yards, it clearly outdistanced all small arms as well as the existing field and mountain artillery. The tube and its wheeled carriage could be towed by a light one-horse limber or readily packed aboard two mules or horses when desirable. Favorably impressed with the little gun, the Ordnance Department purchased one for trial in 1877. Appropriately, the gun with its associated implements and a quantity of ammunition were shipped directly to Miles at Cantonment on Tongue River for field trial.[39]

The Hotchkiss mountain gun performed well enough during the campaign against the Nez Perces that year, though active field service in rough terrain revealed a few deficiencies. On one occasion, according to a soldier in the column, "the little gun, horses and driver were upset down a bank some distance, breaking the pole, but fortunately no one was hurt."[40] Even though the trial gun used a self-contained metallic cartridge, it relied on a friction primer and lanyard for ignition. Gun crews also discovered to their consternation that a significant portion of the ammunition would not chamber properly. Captain Otho E. Michaelis, chief ordnance officer for the Department of Dakota, subsequently recommended that Watervliet Arsenal design a more robust limber made for a two-horse team. More importantly, he suggested that the breech could be modified to incorporate a firing-pin mechanism and that the cartridges be fitted with center-fire primers to render the gun more reliable and faster to reload. As for the oversized cartridge cases, Michaelis could only urge that greater quality control be exercised over the manufacture of the ammunition. Two years later, the army produced under license with Hotchkiss ten more mountain guns of this modified design, thus inaugurating a trend toward breech-loading artillery in the United States service.[41]

The venerable 12-pounder mountain howitzer last saw combat service during the Nez Perce Campaign. Pursuing the tribe through the mountains of Idaho, General Oliver O. Howard commanded a strong column composed of infantry and cavalry, augmented by five batteries of the Fourth Artillery serving as infantry. Howard supplemented his force with a section of mountain howitzers (two) and a pair of Gatling guns. In this exceptional instance, the guns were served by regular artillerymen detailed from the companies. However, soldiers of other branches of service considered the red legs as something of a curiosity. "The red trimmed uniforms of the artillerymen," remarked Trumpeter Ami F. Mulford, Seventh Cavalry, "cast a strange colored glare before your eyes, after looking at the yellow of the cavalry so long."[42]

The Nez Perces, unlike warriors of other tribes, courageously faced the artillery in headlong charges during the two-day Battle of the Clearwater. A cavalry trooper in the fight observed: "They were brave men, and faced a terrific fire of musketry, gatling gun and howitzers."[43] During the first day of the engagement warriors made a determined assault on the battery posted on the bluffs bordering the east side of the river valley. Their intense and accurate rifle fire felled four of the five crewmen at one of the howitzers. Displaying extraordinary courage, the surviving soldier managed to load and fire the gun by lying on his back between the wheels until the Indians withdrew. In another instance when crewmen suffered heavy casualties, First Cavalryman John P. Schorr attested that "we had a mountain howitzer with Civil War ammunition, but none of us could handle it. Finally an infantryman volunteered, and, after getting the range did a lot of damage to the Indians. He had served some time in the artillery."[44]

During the second day's action, the Nez Perces sought shelter in a ravine and began erecting rock breastworks. Observing this activity, an officer standing some distance in front of and below the battery ordered one of the guns to fire on the Indian position. "I was amazed to see the flash of a discharge close behind me," he wrote, "and then came the shell so near over my head that I could have touched it by reaching up, and to my joy the shell exploded right in the place I had indicated."[45] The action ended later that day when the Nez Perces began withdrawing toward their camp in the valley and the troops responded with a general charge, with the Gatlings and the howitzers adding rather ineffective long-range fire on the fleeing villagers.

The following month Colonel Gibbon took up the pursuit of the Nez Perces in western Montana Territory. Leading six companies of his own Seventh Infantry, two troops of the Second Cavalry, and a party of civilian volunteers, Gibbon also took along a mountain howitzer for good measure. The column caught up with and attacked the Indians on 9 August 1877 at their camp on the Big Hole River. Hampered by difficult forested terrain, the crew was unable to bring the howitzer forward in time for the initial assault. However, when warriors counterattacked during the second phase of the battle, the howitzer crew loosed two rounds at the encampment to help cover the troops' withdrawal to the nearby mountainside. Soon thereafter warriors overran the gun position killing one soldier, wounding two, and driving off the others. The Nez Perces then dismantled the howitzer and scattered the parts to prevent its further use by the soldiers.[46]

The year 1877 also witnessed the army's purchase of another recent invention by Hotchkiss, a 1.5-inch (37 mm) revolving cannon. With its five barrels rotating around a common axis, the gun outwardly resembled a Gatling gun, but its mechanism was entirely different. The

Hotchkiss required a crew of only three men—a gunner, a loader, and a man to transport the ammunition from the limber to the gun. It could fire about thirty explosive rounds per minute by dropping single cartridges into the gun's hopper or sixty-eight rounds per minute using special ten-round "feed cases" attached over the hopper. Even though the cannon had a range of about 2,000 yards, it was not of large enough caliber to be effective against defensive works. Nonetheless, it could be devastating against personnel in the open.[47]

Favorable trials of both Hotchkiss guns induced the Ordnance Department to acquire four more revolving cannons in 1879. An observer writing to the *Army and Navy Journal* that year commented: "I saw some good effective target practice with the Hotchkiss at over a mile and a half range." During the next four years the army purchased eight more 1.5-inch revolving cannons, plus one of 40 mm caliber, all of which were sent to the field. The Ordnance Department gradually lost interest in the complex revolving gun but did acquire five more mountain guns in 1884.[48]

Meanwhile, the Ordnance Department was actively seeking a larger caliber breech-loading field gun to replace the antiquated muzzleloaders carried over from the war. An 1883 board of officers designed a 3.2-inch rifle and contracted with the Midvale Steel Works in Philadelphia, Pennsylvania, to manufacture a trial piece. The following year, firing tests totaling 1,800 rounds determined that the gun could throw a 13-pound projectile up to a maximum range of 6,479 yards. At one mile (1,760 yards), the mean deviation of the projectile varied by only 2½ to 3½ feet, a marked improvement over muzzle-loading cannon. The army adopted the 3.2-inch Steel Breech-loading Rifle, as it was officially named, mounted on a steel carriage in 1885. By the end of the Indian campaigns in 1891, the Ordnance Department had 55 of the new guns, none of which saw combat prior to the Spanish-American War, though some appear in photographs taken in the aftermath of the Wounded Knee Massacre.[49]

Fall 1887 witnessed an insurrection on the Crow Indian Reservation in southeastern Montana Territory. The catalyst was a raid staged by a party of young Crows against one of their traditional enemies, the Piegans, residing on the Blackfeet Indian Reservation far to the northwest. However, when Indian agent Henry E. Williams threatened to arrest the perpetrators, a disaffected segment of the tribe led by a young medicine man known as the Sword Bearer, openly defied the agent's authority. Threats against Williams and his employees led to shots fired into some of the agency buildings, causing the alarmed agent to request that troops be sent from nearby Fort Custer to quell the disturbance. Continued unrest, however, prompted the secretary of war to order additional troops to assemble at Crow Agency to arrest the malcontents. Even though Fort Custer had a sizable garrison, Department of Dakota commander Brigadier General Thomas H. Ruger considered it prudent "to concentrate a considerable force in addition to that post, to overawe the tribe, deter any who might be inclined to resist the troops, and better provide . . . for protection of the extended settlements adjacent to the reservation."[50]

Colonel Nathan A. M. Dudley, commanding Fort Custer, provided the core of Ruger's force—six troops of the First Cavalry, bolstered by two Hotchkiss guns. The proliferation of railroads in the developing West facilitated rapid transportation of troops to trouble spots such as this. Late in October, Ruger dispatched a troop of the Seventh Cavalry, three companies of the Fifth Infantry, and two more Hotchkiss guns via rail from Fort Keogh to Custer Station, some forty-five miles north of the agency. From there the troops marched overland to Crow Agency. Additionally, he directed two companies of the Third Infantry at Fort Missoula, Montana Territory, to proceed to the agency. As a safeguard against potential insurrectionist movement to the south, Ruger requested permission to exercise command over two cavalry troops and an infantry company from Fort McKinney, Wyoming Territory, located just across the border in the Department of the Platte.

Communicating through agent Williams, Ruger ordered the entire Crow tribe to assemble near the agency on the Little Bighorn River. On 5 November, he informed the chiefs and other headmen at their camp downstream that they were to surrender the offenders within an hour and a half; otherwise he would use his troops to arrest them. His edict caused many of the villagers to move their tepees nearer the agency buildings for protection in the event of trouble. Near the expiration of the time stipulated, Sword Bearer, leading some 100–150 young men, left the main village and rode across the Little Bighorn Valley, apparently intending to ford the river and gain the plateau on the west side. Dudley and his cavalrymen moved to cut them off, sparking a brisk skirmish near the river.

Just before the cavalry reached the bottomland, one of the gun detachments, posted on high ground east of the river overlooking the main camp, fired three rounds of explosive shell. Private Theodore F. Pfeifer, Fifth Infantry, recalled that "I was on a field piece in command of Lieut. Sam Miller when the cavalry opened fire. We wound up with artillery. Believe me, there was some wool flying and tepees went high that day." Another witness claimed that "one of the shells burst underneath an Indian on a horse blowing them into the air several feet and killing both of them." The record is unclear as to the exact type of Hotchkiss guns used, but one soldier's recollection suggests that one of them may have been a revolving cannon. Former First Cavalry private Charles Ashdown remembered that "the soldiers used a machine gun . . . for the gun would discharge with a loud report and several seconds later the shot would explode."[51] Sword Bearer and seven of his followers were killed, and several more were wounded during the engagement. The Crows killed one trooper and wounded another in the action, after which the cavalry drove the warriors back to that part of the village lying near the agency. The army subsequently rounded up the survivors identified for arrest and sent them off to prison at Fort Snelling, Minnesota. This regrettable confrontation with a tribe that had always been well disposed toward whites, some of whose men had served as scouts during the Sioux War a decade earlier, restored order at the agency and allowed the rightful headmen once again to assume leadership over the people.

Perhaps the most infamous use of artillery came at the final curtain of the Indian wars: the Wounded Knee Massacre. When the so-called Ghost Dance craze swept through the Lakota reservations in South Dakota during 1890, the army assembled an overwhelming force of troops, including the Seventh Cavalry, drawn from garrisons all across the western United States. Also among those summoned was Light Battery E, First Artillery, which arrived late in November from Fort Riley, Kansas. The unit came armed with four Hotchkiss mountain guns.

On 29 December, the day scheduled for disarming Big Foot's band, troops formed a cordon around the designated council area.

Weinert and the gunners of Battery E, 1st United States Artillery.
Library of Congress

Two troops of the Seventh, dismounted, lined the west and south sides, thus separating the assembled warriors from their village and the noncombatants. A mounted troop stood by farther to the east. Officers positioned the battery on an eminence some two hundred yards to the northwest, flanking it on either side with additional soldiers. As troopers began disarming the sullen warriors, the medicine man, a known proponent of the Ghost Dance, harangued the men to resist. Then someone—no one was quite sure who—fired a shot. One officer said that he saw a soldier fall at the same instant. A general melee ensued, with both sides firing at each other at point-blank range. Numerous combatants fell on both sides, including twenty-five or thirty of the Lakota men and nearly as many soldiers, some of them apparently shot by their own comrades standing opposite them. In the confusion, previously unarmed Lakotas retrieved guns and ammunition from hidden caches. Many bullets fired by the Indians passed through the ranks, cutting down not only soldiers but women, children, and elders who were crowded as onlookers just behind the troop formation. Panic quickly ensued as villagers stampeded from the scene and attempted to escape along a road to the west and through an acutely angling ravine.

The surviving cavalrymen turned on their ground and continued shooting down any Indians in view, either in the ravine or on the smoke-enshrouded village site. Dismounted troopers posted on the perimeter of the field east and southeast of the council ground also opened fire on the fleeing people. Meanwhile, the artillery crews on the hill stood by their guns unable to fire for fear of also hitting their own men below. Twenty minutes or so after the first shot, the three troops of the Seventh Cavalry directly engaged withdrew to rally on the hills just behind the battery. Once the troops were out of danger, the gunners had a clear field of fire. The four guns unleashed a deadly volley of canister that thoroughly riddled tepees, wagons, animals, and any humans still present in the village. One of the artillerymen, Private John Comfort, recounted the effect: "Finally the way was clear. Crack-crash went the 4 guns sending their canister tearing into the mass of warriors, squaws, children, & horses. It was a terrible thing to do but the warriors were mixed with the squaws, and were firing rapidly with their Winchesters, and squaws were seen to kill wounded soldiers."[52]

Captain Allyn K. Capron, commanding the battery, lamented that "it was impossible to avoid it [killing noncombatants], as it was impossible to distinguish man from woman; they all seemed to be firing. . . . I continued to shoot at any parties that were shooting at our troops." Capron directed some of his gunners to continue firing canister rounds to suppress fire still coming from the village and ravine areas, while others sent explosive shells at more distant targets. A cavalry trooper related that he witnessed a shell strike a wagon loaded with women and children. "The shell on exploding on the wagon killed or wounded the whole load." Only a baby survived.[53]

After about half an hour, Colonel James W. Forsyth ordered the command to cease firing. As the pall of smoke drifted from the field, "not a live Indian was left in sight," wrote a newspaper correspondent. Mounted troops circled the ravine preventing villagers from escaping westward and forcing them toward Troops C and D deployed along the south side of the ravine. Moving up the wide ravine floor in dismounted skirmish order, K Troop further pressed the Lakotas within an ever-tightening noose. Two dozen or more people sought refuge in a side gulch, where the warriors dug a pit beneath the overhanging head wall as shelter from the close-range fire of three troops of cavalrymen lying prone along either bank. The soldiers were unable to dislodge the warriors, who exposed themselves only briefly to return fire. Second Lieutenant Harry L. Hawthorne and one mountain gun commanded by Corporal Paul H. Weinert advanced from their hilltop position down to the village site, where the detachment opened fire on the pocket. Weinert described what followed:

> A lot of Indians got into a ravine, from which they were shooting with awful effect. . . . I then took my little Hotchkiss down to the entrance of the ravine and blazed away. When I started I had three men. All of the Indians opened fire on us. One of my men went for ammunition and didn't come back. Everybody ran from the mouth of the ravine where I was to the top of and behind a hill about fifty yards away, excepting [his two crewmen]. . . . I kept moving nearer the Indians, and kept on shooting. . . . Lieutenant Hawthorne came toward me . . . when suddenly I heard him say: "Oh my God!" Looking around I saw him lying on his side, and I then knew he had been hit. Hartzog ran to him and carried him back behind the hill. That left me alone with Green. . . . The Hotchkiss was a single-shot affair and had to be pulled off with a lanyard. . . . I kept yelling for a cool gun—there were three more on the hill not in use. Bullets were coming like hail from the Indians' Winchesters. The wheels of my gun were bored full of holes and our clothing was marked in several places. Once a cartridge was knocked out of my hand just as I was about to put it in the gun, and it's a wonder the cartridge didn't explode. I kept going in farther, and pretty soon everything was quiet at the other end of the line.[54]

Even though the event has since been rightly condemned as a massacre of the Sioux, Corporal Weinert nevertheless was awarded the Medal of Honor for his intrepidity and courage under fire.

Although the army was disadvantaged with obsolete muzzle-loading artillery for more than a decade after the Civil War, during that period the Ordnance Department was not unmindful of developments in Europe. The Prussian victory over France in 1871 proved the effectiveness of steel breechloaders. The German firm of Krupp led the advancement toward modern artillery. Others, such as Hotchkiss, quickly followed with their own innovations. By the mid-1870s, it was obvious, even for an isolationist nation like the United States, that the day of muzzle-loading artillery was past. Nevertheless, domestic development of new breechloaders was seriously hampered by a Congress disinclined to authorize an adequate budget to advance such work. The two patterns of Hotchkiss cannons found favor largely because they happened to coincide with the current need for a longer-ranged, comparatively light-weight breechloader better adapted to Indian fighting than the 1841 mountain howitzer. The advent of the Model 1885 3.2-inch gun offers proof that, despite financial restrictions, the Ordnance Department and the artillery branch collaborated to design a modern field piece to supplant the antiquated 12-pounder Napoleon and the 3-inch ordnance rifle. It would remain the principal arm of the field artillery, supplemented by the 1.65 Hotchkiss Mountain Gun, through the Spanish-American War and into the early years of the next century as American forces continued to emerge on the world stage.

NOTES

1. The outbreak of the Civil War saw the Third Artillery stationed on the Pacific Coast, where it had been since 1854–55. In fall 1861, eight companies transferred to the eastern theater of operations, where they were desperately needed to bolster the Union Army. The other four companies remained to defend San Francisco Bay. Company A had the distinction of serving as a light battery, outfitted with 12-pounder mountain howitzers, in Brigadier General James H. Carleton's California Column. Marching from the coast to Tucson, Arizona Territory, in the spring of 1862, Carleton reclaimed the territory for the Union. Continuing eastward toward the Rio Grande in hopes of intercepting an invading force of Texas Confederates, Carleton's men fought and defeated a combined force of Chiricahua and Mimbres Apaches in a sharp encounter known as the Battle of Apache Pass. A section (two howitzers) of Company A participated in the action. Theophilus F. Rodenbough, ed., *The Army of the United States: Historical Sketches of Staff and Line with Portraits of Generals-in-Chief* (1896; reprint, New York: Argonaut Press, 1966), pp.

343–45; Douglas C. McChristian, *Fort Bowie, Arizona: Combat Post of the Southwest, 1858–1894* (Norman: University of Oklahoma Press, 2005), pp. 44, 51, 55–56.

2. Light artillerymen, except drivers who were unarmed, carried the Model 1840 light artillery saber. Sergeants in charge of pieces and caissons also were armed with a revolver. Rodenbough, *Army of the United States*, pp. 325, 372; Francis B. Heitman, comp., *Historical Register and Dictionary of the U.S. Army*, 2 vols. (1903; reprint, Urbana: University of Illinois Press, 1965), 2:607.

3. *Annual Report of the Secretary of War*, 1866, p. 19 (hereafter cited as *ARSW* with the appropriate year).

4. William Y. Chalfant, *Hancock's War: Conflict on the Southern Plains* (Norman, Okla.: Arthur H. Clark Co., 2010), pp. 85, 158, 176–77, 260–65; Robert M. Utley, ed., *Life in Custer's Cavalry: Diaries and Letters of Albert and Jennie Barnitz, 1867–1868* (New Haven: Yale University Press, 1977), p. 46.

5. Utley, *Life in Custer's Cavalry*, p. 119.

6. The units were Light Batteries K, First Artillery; A, Second Artillery; C, Third Artillery; and B, Fourth Artillery. Post Returns, Fort Riley, Kansas, May, 1869, Returns from U.S. Military Posts, 1899–1916, Records of the Adjutant General's Office, Record Group 94, M617, National Archives and Records Administration, Washington, D.C. (hereafter cited as Post Returns with name of post and months).

7. *Army and Navy Journal*, May 8, 1869, p. 598 (hereafter cited as *ANJ* with date of issue).

8. Post Returns, Fort Riley, Kans., April–Aug. 1869. This skirmish occurred on 11 June 1869 on the Solomon River. *Record of Engagements with Hostile Indians within the Military Division of the Missouri from 1868 to 1882* (1882; facsimile reprint, Fort Collins, Colo.: Old Army Press, 1972), p. 21.

9. Post Returns, Fort Riley, Kans., June–Sept. 1870.

10. Ibid., April and May 1871; Rodenbough, *Army of the United States*, p. 326.

11. According to one authoritative source, the mountain howitzer actually was introduced six years earlier and might be more appropriately termed the Model 1835. However, the Ordnance Manual groups it with other howitzers and guns as "Model 1841," which has become the commonly accepted nomenclature. James C. Hazlett, Edwin Olmstead, and M. Hume Parks, *Field Artillery Weapons of the Civil War* (Cranbury, N.J.: Associated University Presses, 1988), p. 134; *Ordnance Manual for the Use of Officers of the United States Army* (1861; facsimile reprint, n.p.: Ordnance Park Corporation, 1970), p. 20. The wood portions of field carriages, limbers, and caissons normally were painted a rather dark shade of olive drab, with the ironwork painted black. It is interesting to note, however, that with the advent of the prairie carriage more than a decade before the Civil War, Colonel Rufus L. Baker, commander of Watervliet Arsenal, applied cream-colored paint to mountain howitzer carriages and attendant equipment bound for service in the West. Writ-

ing to the commanding officer at Santa Fe, New Mexico Territory, in 1850, Baker reasoned that the lighter color would "better reflect the sun rays, considering your desiccating climate." The number of carriages that may have been painted that color is unknown, but the practice probably ceased after Baker's tenure ended in 1851. *History of the Watervliet Arsenal: Sesquicentennial Edition, 1813–1963* (Watervliet, N.Y.: U.S. Army, 1963), p. 31.

12. *Ordnance Manual*, pp. 51–54, 271, 275–76, 280–81.

13. A detailed description of the friction primer is found ibid., pp. 298–99.

14. Corporal Alexander Brown, Second Cavalry, quoted in Jerome A. Greene, ed., *Indian War Veterans: Memories of Army Life and Campaigns in the West, 1864–1898* (New York: Savas Beatie, 2007), p. 89.

15. Lieutenant George M. Templeton diary, April 29, 1867, manuscript collections, Newberry Library, Chicago, Ill. (first quotation) (copy in author's files); Alexander Brown, "Service Experiences," f. 64, Box 10, Don Rickey Papers, Denver Public Library (second quotation) (hereafter cited as Rickey Papers, DPL). Gibson and Littman are quoted in Grace Raymond Hebard and E. A. Brininstool, *The Bozeman Trail: Historical Accounts of the Blazing of the Overland Routes into the Northwest, and the Fights with Red Cloud's Warriors*, 2 vols. bound as 1 (Glendale, Calif.: Arthur H. Clark Co., 1960), 2:68-69, 79.

16. The same soldier described the artillery at Fort Casper as "two formidable looking little brass pieces, each scarcely three feet long, that guarded the flag pole in the center of the parade ground." William F. Hynes, *Soldiers of the Frontier* (n.p., 1943), p. 126.

17. The Napoleon was termed a "light" 12-pounder gun because the piece weighed approximately 600 pounds less than its predecessor, the Model 1841 12-pounder field gun. *Ordnance Manual*, pp. 19, 74, 280, 385; Hazlett et al., *Field Artillery Weapons*, pp. 179, 188. It should be noted that many Napoleon guns that had seen extensive service during the Civil War had enlarged bores, some up to 5.25 inches in diameter. One source attributes worn, uneven bores to heavy use of canister. "Gas pressure and inertia could have caused the canister shot . . . to jam and wedge outward. Increased jamming and increased velocity toward the muzzle reasonably accounts for the taper observed." Accuracy suffered accordingly. Whether the Ordnance Department inspected and measured bores for such wear prior to sending guns to the frontier is unknown. Hazlett et al., *Field Artillery Weapons*, p. 98.

18. The total weight of the Model 1861 ordnance rifle, including the carriage, was only 1,720 pounds. *Ordnance Manual*, pp. 18–19. The misnomer "Rodman" gun is often found in contemporary accounts. The name apparently derived from Thomas Jefferson Rodman, an 1841 West Point graduate and career Ordnance Department officer. So far as can be determined, Rodman played no role in the development of the ordnance rifle but was involved with the design of large cast-iron seacoast

cannon. The exterior shape of the ordnance rifle tube was similar to the Rodman, hence the misnomer. Heitman, *Historical Register*, 1:841; Hazlett et al., *Field Artillery Weapons*, pp. 120 (quotation), 121, 125. 147. The ordnance rifle fired an iron conoidal explosive projectile patented by Benjamin B. Hotchkiss. Case shot and shell utilized either a time fuze or a percussion fuze, also invented by Hotchkiss. The gun was capable of firing canisters, though the rifled bore created rather erratic dispersal of the lead balls. Hazlett et al., *Field Artillery Weapons*, p. 125; John D. Bartleson Jr., "Hotchkiss Percussion Fuze," *Artilleryman* 37 (Winter 2015): 6–7.

19. The majority of the 6-pounders were located at posts with little or no prospect of Indian trouble, such as Fort Leavenworth, Kansas; Forts Ripley and Snelling in Minnesota; and Camp Douglas, on the outskirts of Salt Lake City, Utah Territory. *Outline Descriptions of the Posts in the Military Division of the Missouri* (1876; facsimile reprint, Fort Collins, Colo.: Old Army Press, 1972), pp. 260–62. Even though large numbers of bronze artillery pieces saw service during the Civil War, they had been rendered obsolescent by 1861 with the development of lighter, less costly wrought-iron rifled guns. Hazlett et al., *Field Artillery Weapons*, pp. 120–21.

20. Second Lieutenant J. W. Biddle to Mother, [n.d.] Oct. 1876, Biddle letters, Jerome A. Greene files, Arvada, Colo.; Greene, *Indian War Veterans*, p. 183 (first quotation); Private William G. Wilkerson questionnaire, f. 44, Box 10, Rickey Papers, DPL (second quotation); Lucile M. Kane, ed., *Military Life in Dakota: The Philippe Regis De Trobriand* (St. Paul, Minn.: Alvord Memorial Commission, 1951), p. 41 (third quotation).

21. Douglas C. McChristian, ed., *Frontier Cavalry Trooper: The Letters of Private Eddie Matthews, 1869–1874* (Albuquerque: University of New Mexico Press, 2013), pp. 93–94.

22. Kane, *Military Life in Dakota*, p. 308. Surgeon Washington Matthews shared a steamer down the Missouri River with Private Rhey following his discharge from the army in September 1868. He noted with a professional eye that "the stump was shapely but not doing well as it was amputated very close to the seat of injury." Ray H. Mattison, ed., "Diary of Surgeon Washington Matthews, Fort Rice, D. T.," *North Dakota History* (Jan. and Apr. 1954): 16–17.

23. Quoted in Greene, *Indian War Veterans*, p. 91.

24. Biddle to Mother, [n.d.] Oct. 1876, Biddle letters, Greene files.

25. Rodenbough, *Army of the United States*, p. 373; Keith A. Murray, *The Modocs and Their War* (Norman: University of Oklahoma Press, 1959), pp. 106, 206–22; Peter Cozzens, *Eyewitnesses to the Indian Wars, 1865–1890*, vol. 2, *The Wars for the Pacific Northwest* (Mechanicsburg, Pa: Stackpole Books, 2002), pp. 127 (quotation), 262–67.

26. Bruce R. Liddic and Paul Harbaugh, eds., *Camp on Custer: Transcribing the Custer Myth* (Spokane, Wash.: Arthur H. Clark Co., 1995), pp. 49–50. According

to Second Lieutenant Charles Braden, Seventh Cavalry, the two guns accompanying the expedition were 3-inch ordnance rifles. This has been confirmed by special fuzes recovered from the battlefield. Cozzens, *Eyewitnesses to the Indian Wars*, vol. 4, *The Long War for the Northern Plains*. (Mechanicsburg, Pa.: Stackpole Books, 2004), p. 140 (quotation); personal communication with C. Vance Haines, 29 Oct. 2016.

27. Cozzens, *Eyewitnesses to the Indian Wars*, 2:373–74. During a Chiricahua Apache outbreak in 1881, three batteries of the Fourth deployed to Arizona, where they served only a few weeks before the regiment transferred to the East. Rodenbough, *Army of the United States*, pp. 326, 374.

28. James H. Bradley, *The March of the Montana Column: A Prelude to the Custer Disaster*, edited by Edgar I. Stewart. (Norman: University of Oklahoma Press, 1961), p. 50. General Terry's Dakota Column included a battery of four Gatling guns, two 1-inch caliber and two .50-caliber, under the command of Second Lieutenant William H. Low Jr., Twentieth Infantry. Hugh Hynds narrative, June 27, 1926, typescript, MBAT-1, vertical files, library, Fort Laramie National Historic Site.

29. William F. Zimmer, *Frontier Soldier: An Enlisted Man's Journal of the Sioux and Nez Perce Campaigns, 1877*, edited by Jerome A. Greene. (Helena: Montana Historical Society Press, 1998), p. 75.

30. Moore quoted in Jerome A. Greene, comp., *Battles and Skirmishes of the Great Sioux War, 1876–1877* (Norman: University of Oklahoma Press, 1993), p. 94.

31. Lieutenant J. W. Biddle to Mother, [n.d.] Oct. 1876, Biddle letters, Greene files.

32. The discussion of the Cedar Creek episode is drawn from Jerome A. Greene, *Yellowstone Command: Colonel Nelson A. Miles and the Great Sioux War, 1876–1877* (Lincoln University of Nebraska Press, 1991), pp. 90–104.

33. Edwin M. Brown, "Terror of the Badlands," p. 10, typescript, f. x-7, Box 9, Order of Indian Wars Collection, U.S. Army Heritage and Education Center, Carlisle, Pa.

34. Ibid., pp. 13–14.

35. Greene, *Yellowstone Command*, pp. 165–75, 102–6.

36. Sandy Barnard, ed., *Ten Years with Custer: A Seventh Cavalryman's Memoirs* (Terre Haute, Ind.: Ast Press, 2001), p. 199.

37. Miles quoted in Greene, *Yellowstone Command*, p. 76. During the 1874 Red River War, Miles's column included two Gatling guns and a field piece said to be a 10-pounder Parrott rifle, though the description was likely in error. The gun was more likely an ordnance rifle. The Gatlings, at least, were engaged at the Battle of Mulberry Creek or Salt Fork of Red River, and it was this action that formed the basis for Miles's opinion. Nelson A. Miles, *Personal Recollections and Observations of General Nelson A. Miles* (1896; reprint, Lincoln: University of Nebraska Press,

1992), p. 168; Robert Wooster, *Nelson A. Miles and the Twilight of the Frontier Army* (Lincoln: University of Nebraska Press, 1995), p. 64.

38. *ARSW*, 1878, p. xiii.

39. Ibid.

40. Zimmer, *Frontier Soldier*, p. 97.

41. Michaelis reported that as a field expedient the depot had replaced the original limber with a Gatling gun limber modified to carry 144 rounds of 1.65 Hotchkiss ammunition. Although it sufficed, he considered the improvised vehicle too heavy for the purpose. Captain O. E. Michaelis to chief of ordnance, 30 Apr. 1878, Letters Received, Tongue River Ordnance Depot, Fort Keogh, Mont. Terr., Records of United States Army Continental Commands, 1821–1920, Record Group 393, National Archives & Records Administration; *ARSW*, 1879, p. 23.

42. Ami F. Mulford, *Fighting Indians in the 7th United States Cavalry* (1879; facsimile reprint, Fort Collins, Colo.: Old Army Press, 1970), p. 69.

43. Quoted in Jerome A. Greene, *Nez Perce Summer, 1877: The U.S. Army and the Nee-Me-Poo Crisis* (Helena: Montana Historical Society Press, 2000), p. 81.

44. Cozzens, *Eyewitnesses to the Indian Wars*, 2:358.

45. Quoted in Greene, *Nez Perce Summer*, p. 87.

46. Ibid., p. 136.

47. Appendix O, "Trial of the Hotchkiss revolving cannon, caliber one and one-half inches," *ARSW*, 1877, pp. 609–26; *ARSW*, 1879, p. 23. A 42-mm version of the Hotchkiss revolving cannon was adopted by the United States Navy and navies of several other nations for use aboard warships as a defense against small, fast torpedo boats. wikipedia.org/wiki/Hotchkiss_gun.

48. *ANJ*, 2 Aug. 1879, p. 385 (quotation); *ARSW*, 1884, p. 45.

49. *ARSW*, 1883, p. 13. The 3.2- inch rifle could range a mile with only 3 degrees of elevation. The initial velocity of the shell averaged 1,747 feet per second. *ARSW*, 1885, pp. 494–95. The results of the trials are published in Appendix 49, Report of the Chief of Ordnance, *ARSW*, 1885, pp. 492–99; *ARSW*, 1886, p. 27; *ARSW*, 1887, p. 31; *ARSW*, 1890, p. 41; *ARSW*, 1891, p. 31.

50. Quoted in *ARSW*, 1888, p. 147.

51. "Custer Battle Ground," *Army and Navy Register*, 15 Jan. 1926, p. 5 (first quotation); Richard Upton, *Fort Custer on the Big Horn, 1877–1898: Its History and Personalities as Told and Pictured by Its Contemporaries* (Glendale, Calif.: Arthur H. Clark Co., 1973), p. 150 (second quotation); "Old Soldier Residing Here Tells of Army Life at Frontier Posts," n.d., n.p., Montana Scrapbook, Vol. 1, Montana Room, Parmly Billings Library, Billings, Mont. (third quotation).

52. Quoted in Jerome A. Greene, *American Carnage: Wounded Knee, 1890* (Norman: University of Oklahoma Press, 2014), pp. 235–36.

53. Ibid., p. 236.

54. Quoted in W. F. Beyer and O. F. Keydel, eds., *Deeds of Valor: How America's Heroes Won the Medal of Honor*, 2 vols. (Detroit, Mich.: Perrin-Keydel Co., 1905), 2:325.

4 : **No Time to Fight**

Recreation in the Frontier Army

LORI A. COX-PAUL

Hollywood's depiction of the frontier army of 1865–1900 could lead us to believe that every minute of a soldier's day was spent in heated battle fighting Indians. In reality, his life was usually devoid of fighting or threat of attack. Army posts of the post–Civil War era were often located in remote areas, and the isolation and lack of real soldiering created a need for recreational outlets for the soldiers and their dependents. As Don Rickey, author of the seminal *Forty Miles a Day on Beans and Hay*, wrote, "Isolation, boredom, and monotony characterized life at the western posts."[1] Organized play helped fill the day of the bored soldier, sometimes keeping him away from the less socially acceptable pursuits of drinking, gambling, and whoring.

The frontier army of this period was not the army of the Civil War. It was a ragtag group of men, a third of whom found the hardships of living on the western frontier so miserable that they deserted.[2] When there were no Indian alarms, in addition to following routine fatigue and drill duties, the army had to make work for enlisted men and often used soldiers as common laborers. In some cases, the men were put to service as construction workers and built the very forts where they resided. Other duties included cutting and hauling firewood, transporting water, and cleaning the post. Enlisted man Andrew Flynn recalled one such detail to which he was assigned at Fort Riley, Kansas, in 1888. He noted that a "large detail was set to pull out sunflowers that almost covered the parade ground. Some of the boys were complaining about this, saying, 'I came here to be a soldier.'"[3]

Once the forts were established and Indian troubles abated, peace came to the frontier army. These conditions encouraged officers' wives to move west, and their presence on military posts often influenced recreational activities. Frances Anne Boyd, wife of Lieutenant Orsemus B. Boyd, noted that the men "were ever ready to be amazed or amused . . . with the results of our industry, and absolute delight was manifested over the most trifling plan for social enjoyment."[4]

The many diaries, private letters, official correspondence, newspaper stories, and other first-person accounts offer revealing glimpses into everyday life. The purpose of this essay is to examine these sources, many of them from the northern plains, and review the wide variety of recreational activities of the officers and enlisted men in the frontier arm. With tongue firmly planted in cheek, we could conclude that, contrary to the stereotypical image, the frontier soldier was so busy playing that he simply had no time to fight.

How much fighting was there really? The frontier army engaged in approximately a thousand combat actions between 1866 and 1890 in order to accomplish its mission of protecting the lives and property of the white population who had come to settle the West. Clearly the frontier army was busier fighting in the late 1860s than in the 1880s. The reasons for this are obvious. As Robert Utley observed: "In the year of Wounded Knee four transcontinental railroads spanned the West, where in 1866 there had been none. In 1890, 8.5 million settlers occupied the Indian's former hunting grounds, where in 1866 there had been less than 2 million."[5] Heitman's *Historical Register and Dictionary of the United States Army* shows that the entire trans-Mississippi army saw only twenty-nine days of "battle" in 1878, one year after the surrender of Crazy Horse. By 1884 only one engagement was recorded for the entire year.[6]

Once Indian troubles were largely settled, residents of frontier army posts had ample time to pursue recreational activities. Soldiers frequently chronicled these doings in the *Army and Navy Journal*, a privately owned weekly newspaper founded in 1863, and in the *Army and Navy Register*, a competing publication of similar format established in 1879. As one correspondent from Camp Bidwell, California, reported to the *Army and Navy Journal*:

> Since the settlement of the Modoc question we have had comparative quiet at the post. We formed a club last July called the Bidwell Social Club. Since that time we have built a hall 30×45

and furnished it well. The club subscribe[s] for fourteen different papers; the officers send in their papers, and dumb-bells, boxing gloves, and every thing that will serve to amuse and instruct the troop is there to be found. It is truly a social club. The club gave a grand ball in October with two days' races. The ball was a success, and the cavalry horses won all the honors at the races; citizens no where.[7]

This level of activity was by no means unique. The Fort Stanton Social Club in New Mexico Territory was organized in order to "enliven the dull monotony of garrison duty."[8] Fort Custer, Montana Territory, boasted several clubs, including the Officers' Literary Club, a Masonic Lodge of Instruction, the Custer Social Club, the Ancient Order of Hibernians, Walker's Opera Company, the Fort Custer Comic Opera and Burlesque Company, and also a very exuberant yet sober lodge of the Independent Order of Good Templars.[9] Peacetime led some forts to desire recruits with special qualifications that had nothing to do with soldiering skills. A correspondent from Fort Stevenson, Dakota Territory, wrote only half in jest: "What is badly needed here is material for a string band and a couple of good song and dance 'artists.' When recruits are forwarded I hope the regimental adjutant will think of us in this line."[10]

Sports were popular at all army posts, particularly baseball, football, and boxing. Fort teams competed against men stationed at their posts, soldiers stationed at neighboring forts, and civilian teams from nearby towns. Athletic uniforms and sports equipment were purchased with money from company funds donated by enlisted men and officers. Usually team sports were fielded by enlisted men only, although officers are also occasionally noted as playing. More typically, officers sometimes served in the role of umpire. Such was the case at a baseball game at Fort Omaha, Nebraska, in 1887, where "Lieutenant [William M.] Wright, Second Infantry, was the umpire, and gave complete satisfaction. He is well up on the points of the game and plays an excellent game himself."[11]

At the Cheyenne River Agency, Dakota Territory, located some 250 miles from any city, one correspondent noted in 1871 that "our means of supplying sources of amusement are rather limited. We have, however, a very good base-ball club, at the station, and when the weather is favorable we take a turn at base-ball, which, along with foot and sack races, constitutes our principal source of amusement."[12] According to a correspondent from Camp Lower Brule, South Dakota, in 1890, "Baseball, of course, as a national game, is an epidemical disease among our boys, and several match games have been played in the dreamy interval of camp duties between them and the Sioux and Chamberlain nines which for average good play and gritty reserve . . . showed favorably on the scores for the 'Blues.'"[13] The celebration of Thanksgiving day would not be complete without a good game of football. Fort Sully, Dakota Territory, in 1883 held "a game of football for all hands, two companies on each side. Several of the fellows were fairly well bruised up and your humble servant among the rest. I am now in the hospital on the strength of it."[14] A series of football games between the cavalry and artillery at Fort Riley in 1894 was consistently won by the cavalry, "but not without several injuries to some of the players." The correspondent added that "the sport is almost a brutal one, and doubtless it would be beneficial to the Service and all concerned if the game was not permitted to be played among enlisted men."[15]

Gymnasiums could be found at some of the larger forts. The *Army and Navy Register* mentioned the construction of one such facility at Fort Robinson, Nebraska, in 1888, which included "horizontal bars, ladders, springboards and parallel bars."[16] The gymnasium constructed in 1884 at Vancouver Barracks, Washington Territory, featured an additional attraction, an attached bowling alley.[17]

Equestrian pursuits were extremely popular, particularly at posts garrisoned by cavalry units. Men and women alike enjoyed riding. The *Army and Navy Register* noted in 1887 that at Fort Gibson, Indian Territory, "The young ladies of the post are making heroic efforts to learn to ride horse back, and an occasional fall adds to their experience. We wish them more success and a fewer number of falls."[18] In addition to leisurely riding, several forts, including Fort Davis and Fort Mason in Texas and Fort Leavenworth in Kansas, laid out their own horse racing tracks. Fort Sill, Oklahoma, formed the Fort Sill Jockey Club and hosted its first race in 1870 in front of a crowd of "seven or eight hundred spectators."[19]

Hunting, which became a popular pastime due to the proliferation of wild game located near the forts, also provided the side benefits of honing shooting skills and offering supplements to the meager diet of the frontier army soldiers. "Hunting leaves" were encouraged by the army. One anonymous author in the *Army and Navy Journal* noted the military benefits from such leaves. "They give a minute and practical knowledge of field life and of the country passed over; they teach one to use his rifle with the greatest accuracy and rapidity, and to estimate distances correctly; they give robust health and cheerfulness, and in this way eliminate one of the causes of desertion." In addition, the author noted that "the abundant exercise enjoyed—on horseback in the open air—is just the thing to build up that iron constitution and capacity for endurance which is so necessary and so much to be desired."[20] Suffice it to say, location dictated what the soldiers hunted. In 1875, while taking break for searching for gold, a hunting party was organized by Colonel Richard I. Dodge in which General George Crook and other officers participated. A correspondent wrote of the affair: "The Black Hills would not be [the] Black Hills without getting some game." Their "bag" was "31 deer and elk and one sheep."[21] In 1889, at Fort Duchesne, Utah Territory, "Lieutenants [William C.] McFarland and [James T.] Anderson of the Sixteenth Infantry returned from a very successful hunt. They brought in three wagon loads of venison, which was generously distributed to all in the garrison."[22] At Fort Townsend, Washington Territory, the prey was seafood, as an anonymous correspondent noted in 1884: "When the men have nothing else to do they amuse themselves by digging clams, which are very numerous along the beach. The popular expression here is, 'When the tide is out, the table is set.'"[23]

Shooting contests also served the dual purpose of providing a recreational outlet and improving firearm proficiency. A contest hosted by Fort Meade, Dakota Territory, in 1885 is but one of many examples. The contest was between "ex-First Sergeant M. T. Parham and Sergeant J. W. Umphrey, of the Seventh Cavalry, for $50 a side. As both parties have gained a large reputation as marksmen, this will be an interesting affair. The shooting will be as follows: Five shots at 200 yards, five shots at 300 yards and ten shots at 600 yards."[24]

This example also illustrates that the line between licit and illicit activities was blurred. Sporting events were often combined with gambling. A footrace at Fort McGinnis, Montana, prompted the placing of many bets. As a correspondent to the *Army and Navy*

162 HORSE, FOOT, AND DRAGOONS.

fires melting into the air above. Very gradually the light fades, gray shadows are stealing over the prairie, where the great herd of Agency cattle is slowly moving; the platforms on which the red-skins deposit the bodies of their dead stand out on the mounds black against the sky, and the weird, sobbing wail of mourning women strikes discordantly on our ears. Lights begin to twinkle in the barracks, and, ringing out clear and mellow, the bugle is sounding "first call" for tattoo.

FAIR SHARP-SHOOTERS.

A day or two pass quietly and uneventfully. We visit the range, and waste some ammunition at the big targets with the men, and sometimes, the regular practice over, some of the ladies—no mean shots—join us at the "butts." We roam about the village and Agency, and scrape acquaintance with many of our

Target practice offered an opportunity for the sexes to mingle, as shown in this illustration from Rufus Fairchild Zogbaum's *Horse, Foot, and Dragoons: Sketches of Army Life at Home and Abroad* (New York: Harper & Bros., 1888).

Register reported, "The race, although announced for 2 o'clock, did not occur until about 3. The soldier boys engaged the waiting time, however, in covering all the money thrown in sight by the backers of [Frank] Mills, even offering odds. . . . One fellow was seen fanning himself with a $1,000 bill."[25]

Perhaps in an effort to diffuse the urge to gamble, monetary prizes were sometimes offered as incentives for participation. Lieutenant John Bigelow, stationed in Arizona in 1885, organized a field day for his men on Christmas, whether they wanted it or not. He wrote in his journal:

> At ten o'clock began a series of physical contests among the men, which I had arranged and prepared with no little trouble. I told [the] first sergeant . . . that I wanted to have something of the kind on Christmas day, in lieu of drill, and told him to have some five or six men come to me as a committee. No one came. I asked the sergeant about it the next day, and was told that the men were great growlers. . . . "Some of these men, sir," said the sergeant, "if they go in for anything of the kind, will expect to be excused from duty for a week afterwards." Finding out from him that Cropper and Hazard were still interested, I sent for them. . . . they informed me that some of the men wanted to know, before entering, whether there would be prizes.

Once Bigelow established prize money of $1 per event, he recorded that the field day was successful, with many "participating who had before shown no interest."[26]

Gambling was severely frowned upon by the army. One correspondent viewed it "as the most demoralizing Army vice. Well-raised young men, who come into the Service as sound in mind and body as was Caesar when he crossed the Rubicon, play their way in a very short time to a sure destruction. Schools and reading-rooms for the intellectual advancement of the enlisted men will never accomplish their objects while gambling is openly countenanced and allowed to exist. A game of cards has far more fascination for the average soldier than a lesson in arithmetic, geography, or grammar."[27]

While gambling was not to be tolerated, card games of all sorts flourished. Card playing was probably the most popular off-duty diversion for soldiers, in part because cards could be played anywhere—in the barracks or at the post sutler's store or even in the field while out on campaign.[28] The literature is full of references to poker, whist, and euchre parties. A correspondent to the *Army and Navy Register* wrote that "Captain Geo. D. Wallace, Seventh Cavalry, and wife entertained a number of friends at progressive euchre last Tuesday evening. It was one of the most pleasant and successful parties ever given at Fort Meade."[29] One correspondent considered euchre to be "the fashionable game of cards in the Army," while at Fort Keogh, Montana Territory, in 1888, "bezique seems to be all the rage at cards . . . parties are made up at nearly all the hospitable mansions six times during the week for a whack at this fine, healthy, invigorating sport."[30]

"Fashionable" sporting pursuits were not limited to men. Croquet and lawn tennis were the sports of choice for many officers' wives stationed with their husbands at frontier posts. In 1880 the ladies at Fort Stevenson "laid out a very neat croquet ground, and on pleasant evenings, since the muskeeter has stopped bitin', the scene, with mallets poised and balls flying 'round—generally making targets of the gentlemen's shins—is picturesque and animating."[31] Occasionally croquet was taken up for safety reasons. Margaret Carrington, wife of Colonel Henry B. Carrington and resident of the besieged Fort Phil Kearny, Wyoming Territory, wrote in her 1866 diary: "A game of croquet was planned, and while the ladies could neither ride nor walk beyond the gates, some amusement was attempted between Indian alarms."[32] After Emily McCorkle FitzGerald's physician husband, Dr. Jenkins A. FitzGerald, gave her a croquet set, she commented: "It is a real nice set and as it is the only set at the post, we have enjoyed it ever so much. Doctor says, 'Anything to get you out of doors!'"[33]

Other outdoor diversions included walking parties, picnics, and even a camping trip. A correspondent to the *Army and Navy Register* observed in 1889 that at Fort Snelling, near St. Paul, Minnesota, "walking parties are also greatly in favor and trips to and fro from the city, a distance of seven miles, are often made by four enterprising young ladies, who, needless to say, do not lack for pleasant company on the way."[34] In the summer of 1884, the officers and ladies from Fort Yates and Fort Abraham Lincoln, Dakota Territory, proposed a joint picnic on the banks of the Cannonball River midway between

Croquet at Fort Bridger, Wyoming Territory, 1870s.
U.S. Signal Corps Collection

the two posts. "Both garrisons heartily responded by uniting their camp and garrison equipage and repairing to the spot designated."[35] This outdoor adventure lasted a week.

Recreational activities did not abate in the least with the advent of winter. New diversions presented themselves, including sleighing, skating, and tobogganing. A correspondent wrote from Camp Spokane, Washington Territory, in 1881: "Sleighing is the principal amusement and is always perfect, the snow being so deep and evenly distributed."[36] The elated residents at Camp Bidwell built their own sleigh and recorded that "the snow, the beautiful snow is on hand, in unlimited quantities, and the merry jingle of the bells is heard from morn till night."[37] Residents at Fort Custer could enjoy skating on "two rinks constructed on the parade ground."[38] Fort Snelling boasted that its skating rink was "the finest in the department,

Picnic near Fort Laramie, Wyoming, 1884.
Wyoming State Archives

[and] by the way, is thronged by graceful skaters at all hours."[39] The men and women of Fort Yates enjoyed sledding, according to a correspondent in 1887: "Several of the officers sent to St. Paul early in the season and got toboggans, which have been enjoyed hugely by the ladies and gentlemen of the garrison."[40] Nebraska's Fort Omaha saw the construction of a toboggan slide in 1887, which "begins at the crest of the hill just west of the post . . . and terminates away east of the garrison—well, probably at the Missouri River."[41] When their "delightful sleighing" disappeared due to lack of snow, residents of Fort Abraham Lincoln constructed a roller skating rink, which "is to consist of a birch floor, length one hundred feet exclusive of the dressing rooms. Many a pleasant hour is anticipated in the rapid transit on miniature wheels."[42]

Other indoor activities enjoyed year-round were the numerous hops, balls, germans, cotillions, and fandangos. These dances were often held in conjunction with elaborate holiday celebrations at frontier military posts.[43] From the traditional Thanksgiving and Christmas to the more obscure Arbor Day, holidays provided an excuse to host a party of some sort. However, many posts needed no holiday excuse and hosted such affairs weekly. Many posts actually built special structures to host these parties, and the increasing presence of "hop rooms" reflected their importance in a soldier's life. Creativity flourished at each ball. Efforts were made to vary the theme so that new costumes could be sewn, decorations made, and food prepared.

Apparently, no one ever turned down an opportunity to host a costume ball. As Elizabeth Custer recounted, "A fancy-dress party was always amusing out there, for it was necessary to exercise great ingenuity in getting up costumes. We were masked carefully, and often the dress was such a complete disguise that a husband and wife were kept in ignorance of each other until the signal for unmasking was given at supper."[44] Fort Randall, Dakota Territory, was the setting of a "phantom party," where the participants arrived in sheets.[45] Some of these parties featured extremely elaborate costumes. Fort Yates hosted a "Mikado party" with the guests costumed in "Oriental style."[46] Fort Yates was also the scene of a "tissue paper, fancy dress" party, where the guests dressed in costumes constructed of tissue paper. One female guest came as a sunflower: "the entire costume was made of yellow tissue paper, the skirt of walking length, trimmed with a paper ruffle or flounce. Above these several rows of fringed paper, gracefully hung, surmounted by a border of sunflowers of yellow paper, with brown plush centres." Not to be outdone by the ladies, Captain Thomas M. McDougall of the Seventh Cavalry dressed as the Marquis de Lafayette. "His suit of black, with yellow paper facings, white paper ruffles, knee-breeches and Continental hat was very handsome." The decorations, corsages, boutonnieres, and dancing cards were all fashioned from tissue paper.[47] Fort Sam Houston, located near San Antonio, Texas, hosted a Dickens party, where the guests dressed as characters from his novels.[48] At Fort Meade, a "leap year" party was given on Valentine's Day. The ladies dressed as soldiers, and the soldiers dressed as ladies.[49] On another occasion at Fort Yates, a correspondent noted that "the most gorgeous and prob-

George Custer and family friend Agnes Bates in Indian costume, Fort Abraham Lincoln, 1875. *National Park Service, Little Bighorn Battlefield National Monument*

ably best masqued couple were Lieutenant [Richard C.] Croxton, Fifth Infantry, dressed as a Sioux chief in full feather, with Major James McLaughlin (our worthy Indian agent) as his squaw, and so well did they portray the Indian character that their most intimate friends failed to recognize them."[50] Fort Sidney, Nebraska, hosted a creative dance in 1888, which surely was intended to offer educational benefits. According to the *Army and Navy Register*, "Partners were chosen by lot, the gentlemen being given pieces of paper on which the name of a State was written, and the ladies slips with the names of the State capitals, each gentleman dancing with the lady representing the capital of his State."[51]

Special occasions also served as the backdrop for parties. In 1889, the Fort Yates hop room was the scene of an elaborate party to celebrate the twenty-fifth wedding anniversary of the aforementioned Standing Rock Indian agent James McLaughlin and his wife. "The post hall was brilliantly lighted and tastefully draped with handsome Indian blankets, buffalo robes, and skins of wild animals secured in the chase, presented to the Major by no less than the two great chiefs, Sitting Bull and Gall." The affair included an elaborate supper and dancing that lasted until three in the morning.[52] The sixth birthday party for Emma Spencer, daughter of the post surgeon at Fort Sisseton, Dakota Territory, was noted as being "a delightful surprise in the shape of a birthday party at which older people were not excluded."[53]

Musical and theatrical performances were frequent diversions, in which both enlisted men and officers were able to showcase their talents. While an official army act in 1869 had abolished regimental bands, almost every regiment maintained one, which provided entertainment for concerts, parades, and dances.[54] A correspondent reported that the Eighth Infantry band, stationed at Fort Niobrara, Nebraska, in 1886 "plays at guard mount in the morning and a concert between 2 and 3 o'clock in the afternoon."[55] Often the officers and enlisted men of the regiment provided the monetary support for the band. In 1886 at Fort Meade "about $1,000 has been spent on the band within six weeks in the shape of new instruments, music and paraphernalia."[56] Colonel Benjamin H. Grierson, commander of the segregated Tenth Cavalry and former music teacher, asked the white officers of his command to contribute fifty dollars and each black enlisted man to contribute fifty cents to purchase instruments and sheet music.[57]

Dramatic clubs were organized at most forts. A Fort Keogh correspondent wrote in the *Army and Navy Register* in 1884: "One of the chief sources of amusement at frontier military posts are amateur theatricals. Scarcely any garrison, however small in size or numbers, is without that permanent fixture—a stage and footlights. Indeed I do not hesitate to say that many of our military friends would be surprised, nay, astonished, could they drop in upon some little theater on the plains or nestled among the Rockies and witness the display of histrionic talent that is brought out by isolation."[58]

The military garrison at Standing Rock Agency presented a program with a familiar storyline in 1878, entitled "A Night on the Little Big Horn."[59] Nearby Fort Yates also made an attempt at a historical production in an evening of tableau scenes: "Mrs. [Guy] Howard as Pocahontas saving the life of Captain John Smith, with Lieutenant [Frederick A.] Smith as John Smith, Lieutenant [Palmer G.] Wood, Powhatan, Charles McLaughlin as the Indian executioner with tomahawk in hand, with two real Sioux Indians all in war paint and Indian dresses, feathers and scalping knives, was as a whole simply superb and true to life, and beyond the descriptive power of my poor pen."[60] Most presentations, however, were of an intentionally comic nature. Fort Totten, Dakota Territory, described its winter program for 1871 as featuring "laughable anecdotes, irresistible drolleries, jovial jokes, funny conundrums, and queer sayings."[61]

Even the simplest activities provided diversions. Fort Davis hosted a candy pull in 1887.[62] A Fort Sidney evening featured a cake walk: "A large cake was suspended from the ceiling, and the guests joined in line and marched around the hall to the sweet strains of the Twenty-first Infantry Band."[63]

New technological inventions found their way to most posts. At Vancouver Barracks, a stereopticon was "provided as one of the regular winter amusements for the families at the garrison and their invited guests. On the occasion referred to, a few of the townspeople and the families of the officers were present, and for an hour were very highly edified by exhibitions of statuary, street scenes, and comic sketches."[64] The commander of the Department of the Platte hosted a unique entertainment for Christmas 1877 at Omaha Barracks, using a new invention: the telephone, as the *Omaha Daily Republican* reported. "A telephonic entertainment was given on Thursday evening between the residence of Gen. George Crook, Davenport and 18th streets, and the office of Gen. [John H.] King, post commandant at Omaha Barracks. . . . The programme was impromptu, and not only comprised vocal and instrumental selections, but also a conversation in the Crow language between Gen. Crook and Major [Andrew S.] Burt."[65]

The army probably wished that all of its enlisted men would partake in one recreational endeavor: education. Most army installations did feature post libraries or reading rooms, and some offered classes. In fact, the army eventually required that school facilities be maintained for all enlisted men at permanent stations.[66] Many men could neither read nor write upon their enlistment. A correspondent reported on the Cheyenne River Agency: "The soldiers have a night school here, which is pretty well attended; they receive several standard magazines and newspapers weekly, the most eagerly sought for of which is the *Army and Navy Journal*."[67] As Fort Custer boasted, "Nearly every troop and company in the garrison has a private library."[68] The library at Fort McPherson, Nebraska, contained some 362 books, while Fort Sully more than doubled that with 800.[69] Like the funding of regimental bands, many libraries were funded through assessments or donations to literary societies. At Fort Clark, Texas, however, the physical location of the library made reading somewhat challenging to the soldiers, according to one disconcerted correspondent: "[It] would be well and good if the post hall was not connected with the post library. Every time the hall is taken for entertainments, the members, especially the enlisted men of this garrison, are deprived of their reading that evening. It would be advisable to remove the library to some quiet place, where hops, shows, etc., would not interfere with the reading."[70]

Lectures were also a frequent source of edification. John D. Parker of Fort Riley, Kansas, made an impassioned plea for the value of lectures in 1889 in the *Army and Navy Journal*: "Courses of home lectures at our forts during the winter season would be profitable both to officers and men. Valuable time is lost at our posts which might be made more precious than gold. The tendency toward recreation and amusements some times is too strong. A counter tendency is needed, something bracing and stimulating to the intellectual man. A good lecture is a tonic in life."[71]

The post surgeon was often called to duty in this regard. At Boise Barracks, Idaho Territory, in 1887 surgeon Alfred C. Girard delivered a lecture on the human hand. His audience listened with great interest, especially one Private Douglass, who, ironically, "accidentally shot himself in the left hand the day after the lecture."[72] The post surgeon at Fort Abraham Lincoln offered a series of lectures in 1887. His topics included fractures, dislocations, and sprains; hemorrhages from any cause; drowning: what to do first and how to proceed to resuscitate a drowned person; and burns and scalds. "The doctor is a fluent speaker and shows that he loves his profession."[73] Fort Custer offered a more varied program, including a course of lectures: "Dr. [James E.] Pilcher on the question of the fate of Louis XVI of France. This was followed by lectures by Lieutenant [Frederick K.] Ward, First Cavalry, on the 'Telephone, How It Transmits Speech;' by Lieutenant [George P.] Borden, Fifth Infantry, on Gladstone; by Captain [Moses] Harris, First Cavalry, on 'The First Cavalry in the Shenandoah Valley;' and a paper by Captain [Frank K.] Upham, entitled, 'A Heritage of Crime.'"[74]

In addition to lectures by the post surgeon, officers also shared their personal exploits. Colonel Guy V. Henry "delivered an excellent lecture at Omaha . . . on 'Indians and Indian Campaigns.' He told of Indian life, religion, and superstitions, describing notable campaigns in the Dept. of the Platte, and, upon being pressed, told of the wound he received in the battle of the Rosebud."[75] General Oliver O. Howard, while passing through Fort Robinson in 1882, "treated the garrison to an intensely interesting lecture on the Battle of Gettysburg. A map of Gettysburg with approaches and surrounding[s] was sketched on the black board by Lieut. [Guy] Howard [his son], which assisted both speaker and hearer."[76] Captain John G. Bourke got a little long-winded at Whipple Barracks, Arizona Territory, in his lecture "With General Crook in the Sierra Madre." He spent two weeks preparing his lecture, which "he inflicted upon the unfortunate people of Prescott last night. You ought to have heard the snoring. Half the audience were asleep in twenty minutes. When I stated that I would not detain them longer, the applause was deafening."[77]

It seems clear that recreational activities of all sorts became a

Masquerade ball at Fort Assiniboine, Montana, 1891.
American Heritage Center, University of Wyoming

prominent feature in the lives of frontier army soldiers. They provided much-needed stimulation and at least offered the men a choice to keep them away from illicit pursuits. In some cases, the activities supplemented their military training or afforded opportunities for self-improvement. As one anonymous army officer's wife wrote in the *Army and Navy Register* in 1888, "The monotony of the Army on the frontier, both for officers and men, is its crying evil. . . . It is plainly the duty of commanding officers and company commanders to vary the monotony by encouraging and proposing amusements for enlisted men."[78]

Many pastimes commonplace in the East were transplanted to the West, but a Fort Bliss, Texas, correspondent championed the army's own unique efforts at recreation:

> There is no entertainment which can compare to that of an army post. No hop-room can be so fascinating as one draped in the long, heavy flags which always form the chief decoration. There is no music as delightful as that of a trained military band, and no citizen's dress-suit ever made could hold its own against the blue uniform and white stripes of the officers' full dress. No woman in the Army is ever a wall-flower. No matter how old she is, whether married or single, she always has the best dancers in the room ask her for one dance at least, and if she is pretty and attractive she is as much of a belle as in the palmiest days of her girlhood.[79]

A Fort Keogh correspondent went further:

> Army people left to themselves on the frontier create amusements and pleasures for themselves which never would be dreamed of were they dwellers of the Atlantic or Pacific slopes. The officers and ladies of our little Army, although isolated from society and all its seductive attractiveness, yet are not entirely without means of enjoyment and recreation, and yearn far less for civilization and all its drawbacks than many would at first suppose.[80]

The sheer volume of primary source material available on recreation and the frontier army offers historians a plethora of further research topics. Any one of the numerous subjects surveyed here warrants more study. There is plenty of source material to go around. Those interested in researching these topics may very well find that they have no time to write.

NOTES

1. Don Rickey, *Forty Miles a Day on Beans and Hay: The Enlisted Soldier Fighting the Indian Wars* (Norman: University of Oklahoma Press, 1963), p. 88. For other detailed analyses of the frontier army that were helpful to this study, *see also* Edward M. Coffman, *The Old Army: A Portrait of the American Army in Peacetime, 1784–1898* (New York: Oxford University Press, 1986); David Dary, *Seeking Pleasure in the Old West* (New York: A. A. Knopf, 1995); John P. Langellier and Cameron Laughlin, *Soldiers at Play: Recreation and Pastimes of the Frontier Army* (Fort Leavenworth, Kans.: U.S. Army Command and General Staff College, 1984); Douglas C. McChristian, *Regular Army O!: Soldiering on the Western Frontier,*

1865–1891 (Norman: University of Oklahoma Press, 2017); Patricia Y. Stallard, *Glittering Misery: Dependents of the Indian Fighting Army* (Norman: University of Oklahoma Press, 1978); Michael L. Tate, *The Frontier Army in the Settlement of the West* (Norman: University of Oklahoma Press, 1999); William A. Dobak, "Licit Amusements of Enlisted Men in the Post–Civil War Army," *Montana The Magazine of Western History* 45 (Spring 1995): 34–45; and Marion M. Huseas, "'Tuched Nothing to Drink . . .': Frontier Army Leisure," *Periodical: Journal of the Council on America's Military Past* 12 (Jan. 1981): 11–23. In addition, the late John D. McDermott generously shared his extensive clippings files from the *Army and Navy Journal* and *Army and Navy Register* with me. Today researchers can easily gain access to digitized versions of the *Army and Navy Journal* online at catalog.hathitrust.org/Record/008898673.

2. John D. McDermott, "Were They Really Rogues?: Desertion in the Nineteenth-Century U.S. Army," *Nebraska History* 78 (Winter 1997): 166. McDermott chronicled different methods used to calculate desertion statistics. See also Robert M. Utley, *Frontier Regulars: The United States Army and the Indian, 1866–1891* (New York: Macmillan Publishing Co., 1973), pp. 23–24.

3. Quoted in Jerome A. Greene, *Indian War Veterans: Memories of Army Life and Campaigns in the West* (New York: Savas Beatie, 2007), p. 184.

4. Orsemus Bronson Boyd, *Cavalry Life in Tent and Field* (New York: J. Selwin Tait and Sons, 1894), p. 146.

5. Utley, *Frontier Regulars*, p. 420.

6. Francis B. Heitman, *Historical Register and Dictionary of the United States Army, from Its Organization, September 29, 1789, to March 2, 1903*, 2 vols. (Washington, D.C.: Government Printing Office, 1903), 2:444, 447.

7. *Army and Navy Journal* (hereafter *ANJ*), 3 Jan.1874, p. 324.

8. *Army and Navy Register* (hereafter *ANR*), 24 Dec. 1887, p. 820.

9. *ANR*, 24 Feb. 1886, p. 259.

10. *ANR*, 16 Oct. 1880, p. 1.

11. *ANR*, 26 Sept. 1887, p. 564.

12. *ANJ*, 13 May 1871, p. 619.

13. *ANJ*, 9 Aug. 1890, p. 930.

14. Quoted in Harold H. Schuler, *Fort Sully: Guns at Sunset* (Vermillion: University of South Dakota Press, 1992), p. 165.

15. *ANJ*, 13 Jan. 1894, p. 350.

16. *ANR*, 28 Jan. 1888, p. 62.

17. *ANR*, 1 Mar. 1884, p. 9.

18. *ANR*, 20 Mar. 1887, p. 341.

19. Anne Bruner Eales, *Army Wives on the American Frontier: Living by the Bugles* (Boulder, Colo.: Johnson Books, 1997), p. 81; *ANJ*, 22 Oct. 1870, p. 155

(quotation). I have covered this topic in further detail in a paper entitled "Horsing Around: Recreational Uses of Horses in the Frontier Army," at the Sixth Fort Robinson History Conference, Crawford, Nebraska, 26–28 Apr. 2007.

20. *ANJ*, 12 July 1884, p. 1023. For an in-depth treatment of hunting in the frontier army period, *see* James E. Potter, "'The Great Source of Amusement': Hunting in the Frontier Army," *Montana The Magazine of Western History* 55 (Autumn 2005): 34–47.

21. *ANJ*, 21 Aug. 1875, p. 21.

22. *ANR*, 21 Dec. 1889, p. 703.

23. *ANR*, 16 Feb. 1884, p. 4.

24. *ANR*, 30 May 1885, p. 345.

25. *ANR*, 13 June 1885, p. 375.

26. John Bigelow Jr., *On the Bloody Trail of Geronimo* (Los Angeles: Westernlore Press, 1958), pp. 99–100.

27. *ANJ*, 16 Oct. 1880, pp. 201–2.

28. Rickey, *Forty Miles a Day*, p. 209.

29. *ANR*, 14 Apr. 1888, p. 229.

30. *ANR*, 7 Feb. 1885, p. 93; *ANR*, 24 Mar. 1888, p. 189 (quotation).

31. *ANJ*, 16 Oct. 1880, p. 201–2; *ANR*, 16 Oct. 1880, p. 1 (quotation in both sources).

32. Margaret Carrington, *Ab-sa-ra-ka, Home of the Crows: Being the Experience of an Officer's Wife on the Plains* (Philadelphia: J. B. Lippincott and Co., 1869), p. 163.

33. Emily McCorkle FitzGerald, *An Army Doctor's Wife on the Frontier* (Pittsburgh: University of Pittsburgh Press, 1962), p. 135.

34. *ANR*, 9 Feb. 1889, p. 84.

35. *ANJ*, 16 Aug. 1884, p. 43.

36. *ANJ*, 26 Mar. 1881, p. 699.

37. *ANJ*, 3 Jan. 1874, p. 324.

38. *ANR*, 19 Jan. 1889, p. 39.

39. *ANR*, 9 Feb. 1889, p. 84.

40. *ANR*, 19 Mar. 1887, p. 180.

41. *ANR*, 31 Dec. 1887, p. 831.

42. *ANJ*, 28 Mar. 1885, p. 693.

43. For a lengthy treatment on the celebration of Christmas at frontier army forts, *see* Lori A. Cox-Paul and James W. Wengert, *A Frontier Army Christmas* (Lincoln: Nebraska State Historical Society, 1996). I expounded on this topic in "A Frontier Army Fourth and Other Holidays," presented at the Order of the Indian Wars Symposium, Denver, Colorado, 19 Apr. 2008.

44. Elizabeth B. Custer, *Boots and Saddles: Or, Life in Dakota with General Custer* (Norman: University of Oklahoma Press, 1961), pp. 182–83.

45. *ANR*, 31 Mar. 1883, p. 14.
46. *ANR*, 11 Sept. 1886, p. 580.
47. *ANJ*, 17 Jan. 1885, pp. 487–88.
48. *ANR*, 9 Mar. 1889, p. 148.
49. *ANJ*, 17 Mar. 1888, pp. 675–76.
50. *ANR*, 31 Dec. 1887, p. 836.
51. *ANR*, 11 Feb. 1888, p. 84.
52. *ANR*, 9 Feb. 1889, p. 84.
53. *ANJ*, 27 February 1886, p. 620.
54. Utley, *Frontier Regulars*, p. 91.
55. *ANR*, 20 Dec. 1886, p. 820.
56. *ANR*, 30 Oct. 1886, p. 692.
57. Eales, *Army Wives*, p. 85.
58. *ANR*, 17 May 1884, p. 5.
59. *ANJ*, 13 Apr. 1878, p. 568.
60. *ANR*, 30 Mar. 1889, p. 196.
61. *ANJ*, 4 Mar. 1871, p. 461.
62. *ANR*, 5 Mar. 1887, p. 148.
63. *ANR*, 12 Jan. 1889, p. 18.
64. *ANR*, 18 Dec. 1880, p. 1.
65. *Omaha Daily Republican*, 22 Dec. 1877.
66. Rickey, *Forty Miles a Day*, p. 194.
67. *ANJ*, 13 May 1871, p. 619.
68. *ANR*, 24 Feb. 1886, p. 259.
69. Eales, *Army Wives*, p. 86.
70. *ANR*, 21 Apr. 1888, p. 244.
71. *ANJ*, 16 Feb. 1889, p. 497.
72. *ANR*, 16 July 1887, p. 459.
73. *ANR*, 18 June 1887, p. 388.
74. *ANR*, 20 Mar. 1886, p. 178.
75. *ANJ*, 17 Dec. 1887, p. 398.
76. *ANJ*, 4 Nov. 1882, p. 306.
77. *ANJ*, 28 Feb. 1885, p. 606.
78. *ANR*, 10 Nov. 1888, p. 708.
79. *ANJ*, 19 Feb. 1887, p. 591.
80. *ANR*, 17 May 1884, p. 5.

5 : "A Very Good Friend to the Army"

The Frontier Soldier in the Western Art of Frederic Remington

BRIAN W. DIPPIE

At the end of December 1895, Major General Nelson A. Miles paid Frederic Remington a telling compliment in a letter of introduction sent from Army Headquarters, Washington, D.C., addressed to Department and Post Commanders: "This will introduce Mr. Frederic Remington, who has been a very good friend to the Army, and who now desires to visit some of the Western posts on a tour of sketching. Any courtesies extended to him will be highly appreciated by him and myself." As a budding illustrator for *Harper's Weekly*, Remington had first met Miles while covering the Geronimo campaign in 1886. Subsequently he had close contact with the general during the Ghost Dance War in 1890, traveled with him to Mexico to sketch the army in the spring of 1891, frolicked with him on a bear hunt in the Rockies in 1893, and cheered on Miles's troops against the Pullman strikers in Chicago in 1894, agreeing that it was time the protesters learned "a first lesson by the bayonet and the bullet." Miles recognized that Remington's strong conservative views and large following made him valuable as an advocate for the army and an ally in advancing his own career.[1]

Fittingly, in 1896 Miles chose Remington to illustrate his self-promoting *Personal Recollections and Observations*, an oversize tome "embracing" the thrilling "story of his Indian campaigns." When Miles called Remington "a very good friend to the Army," he was appearing regularly in some of the leading periodicals of the day—*Harper's Weekly*, *Century*, *Harper's Monthly*, *Cosmopolitan*, *Outing*, *Scribner's*—and had already planted enduring images of western life in the public's mind. Many of them paid tribute to the sacrifices

"General Miles and his Escort," *Harper's Weekly* 34 (6 Dec. 1890).

and hardships of military duty on the remote frontier and the stirring heroism in battle of the "boys in blue." These are Frederic Remington's frontier soldiers—*our* frontier soldiers, because his direct, unblinking style was so persuasive that it made illustrations artfully cobbled together from observation and imagination seem like unembellished documents. As Owen Wister wrote in 1902, Remington "has taken the likeness of the modern American soldier and stamped it upon our minds with a blow as clean-cut as is the impression of the American Eagle upon our coins in the Mint."[2]

Born in Canton, New York, in October 1861, Frederic Remington, the only child of Clara and Seth P. Remington, grew up relishing outdoor activities like canoeing and camping and tramping in the woods. He was daft about soldiers and horses. Like others of his generation who were too young to participate in the Civil War, he heroworshipped his father, who had served as an officer with the Eleventh New York Cavalry Regiment. He was Remington's soldierly ideal—a battle-tested manly man, at ease with himself, exuding confidence and competence, in every way a model to emulate. Remington attended military schools, then Yale in 1878–79, where his studies in art were secondary to football—and football was a taste of war. The year after his father's death in 1880, Remington made his first trip

"Marching in the Desert," *Century Magazine* 37 (Apr. 1889).

to the West. It seemed to him a substitute battlefield, a setting for great adventure and his own manly challenges. He would visit frequently thereafter as an artist/correspondent. Except for brief residences in Kansas and in Kansas City, New York and Connecticut remained home until his death in December 1909. Remington was an easterner, then, who interpreted the West for a likeminded largely eastern audience.

Alvin H. Sydenham, a cavalry lieutenant who met Remington in 1890 "on the dusty, alkaline banks of the Tongue river, among the Montana foot-hills of the Big Horn mountains," recalled his first impressions of "a fat citizen dismounting from a tall troop horse":

> The horse was glad to get rid of him, for he could not have trained down to two hundred pounds in less than a month of cross country riding on a hot trail. . . . Tending still more to impress the observer with the idea of rotundity and specific gravity was a brown canvas hunting coat whose generous proportions and many swelling pockets extended laterally, with a gentle downward slope to the front and rear, like the protecting expanse of a brown cotton umbrella. And below, in strange contrast with the above, he wore closely fitting black riding breeches of Bedford cord, reenforced

with dressed kid, and shapely riding boots of the Prussian pattern, set off by a pair of long shanked English spurs.[3]

The lieutenant's point is fair: Remington might fancy himself a rough-hewn western outdoorsman, but he was an eastern dandy too. Exactly that was the source of his popular appeal: he was "one of us," and yet he could also manage, even flourish, "out there." By personifying the West, Remington made the remote accessible to eastern readers. So rapid was his rise to prominence as an illustrator and an essayist that a journalist by 1892 could say: "In his pictures of life on the plains, and of Indian fighting, he has almost created a new field in illustration, so fresh and novel are his characterizations. . . . It is a fact that admits of no question that Eastern people have formed their conceptions of what the Far-Western life is like, more from what they have seen in Mr. Remington's pictures than from any other source, and if they went to the West or to Mexico they would expect to see men and places looking exactly as Mr. Remington has drawn them."[4]

Other puff pieces in the journals for which Remington illustrated made similar points: Remington's West had become the real West in people's minds. Like General Miles, Remington was never overmodest and was fully conscious of his standing in the world. Given to sniffing at the unwashed masses, workers and "new Americans" alike, he embodied the sense of Anglo-Saxon superiority rampant among the American upper class at the end of the nineteenth century. He might venerate the common soldier, but he ate and slept with the officers and enjoyed keeping company with the top brass like General Miles. That meant agreeable perks on his western excursions—private rail cars, good champagne, all the privileges of high rank. As an artist/correspondent, he especially favored the company of young officers active in the field and with the sap still rising. If they manifested a touch of arrogance and exhibited an attitude of disdain for their desk-bound elders, all the better when it came to having them strike a pose for his pencil.

Lieutenant Powhatan H. Clarke of the Tenth Cavalry met his every requirement. They first shook hands in Arizona Territory in 1886. Remington made an illustration from hearsay of Clarke's daring rescue of one of his troopers, Corporal Edward Scott, wounded in a skirmish with Apaches. It was published as the frontispiece in *Harper's*

“Lieut. Powhatan H. Clarke, Tenth Cavalry,”
Harper’s Weekly 34 (22 Mar. 1890).

"Soldiering in the Southwest: The Rescue of Corporal Scott,"
Harper's Weekly 30 (21 Aug. 1886).

"Arrival of a Courier," *Century Magazine* 41 (Mar. 1891).

Weekly on 21 August that year. Subsequently, Remington rode with Clarke's troop on a demanding but uneventful two-week patrol from Fort Grant in Arizona, an experience he wrote up and illustrated for *Century* in 1889 as "A Scout with the Buffalo-Soldiers." The Tenth was an African American regiment, though its officers like Clarke were white. Remington included Clarke in an 1890 painting, *Arrival of a Courier*, where he is identifiable by a supercilious, almost insolent, attitude that does not quite disguise a vitality that assures the viewer that this is a man full of vinegar and not to be trifled with.[5]

For Remington, young officers like Clarke were the men who *did* things. Artists merely observed, and recorded, what was before them. After Clarke got him elected to a life membership in the Cavalry Association in 1890, Remington wrote:

> I suppose there must be some perquisites for a member of the Cav. Ass'tion. I'll be blowed if you can ever make me walk up hill like a dough boy, now that I am a cavalryman. Of course my acceptance of this honor is conditioned on the understanding that I am not to

> go to war. My business in life, as a painter and illustrator is to give other fellows the credit that is due for gallantry—I desire no honors of this kind myself. In the public judgment of to day I am accorded the benefit of a doubt as to the heroism of my moral nature and I never want to get up very close to an evily disposed person with a gun for fear that the doubt might be dissipated.

Who Remington was dictated *how* he showed the frontier soldier. With that in mind, we can turn to his major themes.[6]

In June 1876, when George A. Custer perished leading five companies of the Seventh Cavalry at the Little Bighorn, fourteen-year-old Fred Remington was about to enroll as a cadet at Highland Military Academy in Worcester, Massachusetts. He was also an aspiring artist, so depicting Custer's demise was simply irresistible. Drawing on an illustration by Alfred R. Waud in a popular biography of Custer rushed into print that very fall, Remington created his own version of Custer's last fight. The power of Waud's image resided in its pyramidical arrangement of figures, with Custer's head at the apex. The composition was elemental and effective. It impressed itself on Remington's visual memory. He would return to it frequently when addressing related subjects in his mature art showing trappers, cowboys, and soldiers at bay, hardy, fearless men surrounded by circling Indians and prepared to sell their lives dearly. The desperate stand distilled in a single image Remington's great theme, the Winning of the West—for him, a heroic enterprise that had forged a masterful race and a colossus among nations ready to take on the world. Waud's composition is clearly echoed in Remington's double-page illustration in *Harper's Weekly*, published within two weeks of the battle of Wounded Knee, titled with blunt force *The Last Stand*. Desperate "last stands" like this one conveniently reversed historical reality. Indians, after all, were the ones at bay, their lands invaded, their way of life imperiled. The civilization that Remington championed was the aggressor, not the victim. As a field artist covering the Ghost Dance War for *Harper's Weekly* in December 1890, Remington was nearby when some 200 men, women, and children of Big Foot's band of Lakotas were killed at Wounded Knee. Remington was fully aware of the tragic human cost from what he learned from others after the fact. Still, *The Last Stand* appeared in the *Weekly* just twelve days

"The Last Stand," *Harper's Weekly* 35 (10 Jan. 1891).

after Wounded Knee, accompanied by an editorial note that asked: "How many scenes of which this is typical have been enacted on this continent, who can say?"[7]

The concept of *typicality* is essential to understanding the vast influence of Remington's imagery. The illustrator's craft required an ability to generalize convincingly and to populate pictures with generic types made real through repetition. His specialty, of course, was western types—mountain men, vaqueros, packers, miners, Indians—with cowboys and soldiers most prominent among them. In 1891, after painting a horse race, he made his artistic preferences clear to Clarke: "I like cow-punchers & sogers, . . . other things are irksome." His cowboys were sun-burnt, hardy "men with the the bark on," "gems" to Remington (to quote his words). But soldiers were his bread and butter—wasp-waisted, cocky, and masterful. An admiring 1891 *Century* magazine article recounting "General Miles's Indian Campaigns" was illustrated with a Remington drawing titled *A Typical Trooper*—a typical Remington drawing, one might add. It was no great distance from a likeness of Powhatan Clarke to any

"A Typical Trooper," *Century Magazine* 42 (July 1891).

Remington cavalry officer. A bit of Seth Remington lurks inside every one of them. It was by linking his *types* to *typical* action that Remington composed his major paintings—frontier epics of do-or-die. The typical, naturally, had interchangeable parts, subject to subject. Repeated often enough, the typical became the real—indeed, more real than "reality." "In a word, he has fixed on the dial of time types that are disappearing from our Western borders and of which we shall have no other equally satisfactory likenesses," a journalist wrote in 1896. "It is in the essential truth of his records that Remington's drawings will be valuable hereafter. . . . He has made them live, so that we all feel that we know familiarly the cavalryman, the scout, the cowboy, the ranchman, the miner, the broncho, as if we had lived among them."[8]

As if we had lived among them—that precisely was Remington's great power. He was utterly convincing. It was a truism in his day that he was the West's peerless pictorial historian, leaving behind an unvarnished record of what he saw and knew. "He is the most conscientious of historians; he has never 'faked' an action, a costume or an episode," read a typical tribute written a few years before his death. Of course, the exact opposite was true. Remington was not bound by facts. In that sense he "faked" all of his celebrated action pictures showing gunfights and Indian battles and desperate Last Stands. He was an artist, after all, not a historian. And as an artist he was no soldier, as he told Clarke—and he never wished to confuse the two.[9]

Consider what Remington saw—and did not see—out West. He saw cowboys saddling and mounting their horses for a day's work with cattle, not slaughtering one another in a saloon shootout over a misdeal at cards. He saw reservation Cheyennes in Indian Territory chasing down steers with pistols on ration day, not an epic buffalo hunt with an enraged bull tossing an Indian rider and his pony into the air. And when it came to soldiers, he saw troopers on a grueling scout in Apache country who enountered nothing more hostile than the terrain itself and fought no battles to the death of the sort he liked to portray. Granted, Remington did not see any real *action* out West. How about the soldier's everyday routine? Quiet scenes of cavalry in the field were far closer to his personal experience, but even these went through the Remington filter. He sketched episodes showing hardships and mishaps on patrol with the Tenth Cavalry.

"A Campfire Sketch," *Century Magazine* 37 (Apr. 1889).

But the paintings he worked up from those sketches, seemingly documentary in intent, must be understood as artistic contrivances—fabrications, really.

Nothing could seem more faithful to fact than an oil painting done about 1892, *A Cavalryman's Breakfast on the Plains*, showing a scout reporting to officers seated around a campfire taking their morning meal. Despite its documentary aura, however, it was actually cobbled together from several field sketches, not a single source, and the finished product transformed direct observation into an imaginary construct that altered reality. The central group in the painting combined Remington's portrait of *Ben Clark, Interpreter*, published in *Century* in 1889, and a drawing published in *Century* the same year of African American troopers relaxing over coffee, *A Campfire Sketch*. Remington had patroled with black soldiers and sketched them in the field. But in his major paintings the West would be a white man's domain, and in work intended for exhibition black troopers faded out of the picture—or, more accurately, faded to white. They were there, but in a different, more acceptable guise. His "reality" replaced the reality that he had actually witnessed and, through the power of art, became reality for countless others. So what does it mean to say Remington was the "pictorial historian" of the Old West?[10]

In his own work by 1900 Remington aspired to move beyond illustration—pictures usually done in black and white intended for reproduction with an accompanying text—to paintings in color intended as stand-alone works of art, rooted not in words requiring embellishment but in his imagination—"Art" with a capital "A." He craved critical acceptance as a painter and sculptor, and it would not be granted if he were viewed principally as an illustrator. Throughout his career, beginning in 1887, he had exhibited in New York and elsewhere, in a bid to woo the public and court the critics. As he left illustration behind in the twentieth century, he gained ground with the art establishment. Finally, in 1908, after his annual exhibition at Knoedler's in New York, he was able to write a friend: "My show made a great hit this winter and I did pretty well. I am no longer an illustrator."[11]

Along the way, Remington could be inconsistent, feuding with other artists who received critical acclaim and dared to poach on his western domain, attacking them as pretenders who did not know a cavalry boot from a saddle and were thus disqualified—not, it should be noted, as artists but as pictorial historians. The West was still his turf and rivals were not welcome, as Charles Schreyvogel learned when he ruffled Remington's feathers in 1903 with a well-received historical oil, *Custer's Demand*, showing an 1869 parley on the southern plains between Kiowa leaders and General Custer and his staff. Remington by then harbored the belief that Schreyvogel's cavalry and Indian paintings were mostly cribbed from his work, derivative, and thus undeserving of the coveted Clarke Prize awarded the painting *My Bunkie* in 1900 by the National Academy of Design, which never extended such an honor to Remington.

The squabble was all Remington's—Schreyvogel stayed above the fray, letting others defend his painting's accuracy, in the process exposing Remington as jealous and vindictive. He wanted it both ways, after all—his old reputation as the army's "good friend" and the West's preeminent pictorial historian as well as his new standing as a fine artist worthy of the critical recognition at last coming his way. So he launched an unwise attack, dismissing Schreyvogel's painting as "half baked stuff." Nothing was too petty to escape Remington's notice: the pistol holders, ammunition belts, warbonnets, hats, boots, stirrup covers, saddle bags, uniform colors, even the height of Custer's horse—all wrong, all inaccurate! The denouement came when an army officer who was actually present at the parley depicted, the general's widow, Elizabeth Custer, and President Theodore Roosevelt—whose work on ranching and hunting in the West Remington had illustrated—rallied to Schreyvogel's defense, leaving Remington to limp away, looking foolish. Never again would he make such a public issue of historical accuracy. He had learned his lesson and increasingly distanced himself from his popular reputation as a presenter of unadorned fact who had lived what he showed. Indeed, when a journalist in 1908 thought to write up his life, he pleaded, "consider my Art and not myself. I hope the Art is interesting but I assure you I am not."[12]

After the Ghost Dance War of 1890–91, Remington was left without compelling military subject matter set in the West. There were no more Geronimos, no more Sioux outbreaks and celebrated representatives of Indian resistance like Sitting Bull. Remington might no longer care to be thought of as the frontier army's pictorial historian, but a modern peacetime army was even less appealing. It lacked visual interest. Remington covered exhibitions of riding, demonstrations of weaponry, sabre charges and the like—routine field training exercises, in short. Admittedly, preparedness was important, but it did not make for inspiring pictures, and it did not inspire Remington. He branched out to cover foreign soldiers including the French, Prussians, Cossacks, and even Bedouins. But Remington was necessarily treading well-worn ground, and as an American patriot his heart remained at home. "No honey—," he wrote his European traveling companion in 1897, "I shall not try Europe again. I am not built right. I hate parks, collars, cuffs, foreign languages, cut and dried stuff. . . . Europe is all right for most everybody but me. I am going to do America—it's new—it's to my taste." Then, in 1898, it all came together. America went to war against the Spanish in Cuba. Remington, serving once again as a field correspondent, was on hand for the "big murdering." He had always craved a chance to see *real* war—and now that he had it, he was appalled. War was sick and dying men, terrible wounds inflicted from a distance, mud and heat, dirt and disease, and suffering—not at all the glorious contest he had envi-

"The Last March," 1906. *Frederic Remington Art Museum, Ogdensburg, N.Y.*

sioned in his art. Following his rigorous scout with Clarke's Tenth Cavalry in 1888 he had been willing to concede that "soldiers, like other men, find more hard work than glory in their calling." But he was exhilarated, not disillusioned, by the experience and still found glory enough in soldiering to occupy his brush for years. After Cuba, however, reconciling combat as he once imagined it with the reality of what the men who did things actually *do* was much harder than before.[13]

Remington returned from Cuba a chastened man. "As Miss Columbia said to Uncle Sam, 'That was my War'—that old cleaning up of the West—that is the War I am going to put in the rest of my time at," he wrote to Owen Wister in 1899. He explained himself further in a 1907 interview: "Frankly I know nothing about the army as it is right now. I have had nothing to do with soldiers since the war in Cuba. I only knew the soldiers as a part of my West, and the West and the soldier closed together. The uniformed fighting man passed on and off my [drawing] board a long time since." This was a revealing statement in line with something that he had said much earlier. Writing to Powhatan Clarke, his beau ideal, in 1890, he had observed:

"D—— the future—soldiers by profession deal with the future—artists deal with the past though. I dont care a d—— what you cavalrymen are going to do—its what you have done."[14]

After Remington's return from Cuba, even his Old West grew darker, his work moodier and more introspective. Nocturnes, such as *The Last March*, became a speciality, divided between moonlights and firelights as the source of illumination, while night shadows bordered what lay hidden beyond and expressed his recognition that *his* West had been encircled, closed in, and lost in the process of being won. These night scenes were essential to his bid for critical recognition as a pure painter. They did not tell a clearcut story, thus establishing their distance from illustration. In them, he perfected the "art of leaving out." "Big art is a process of elimination," he explained in 1903. "Cut down and out— . . . let your audience take away something to think about—to imagine." Night cloaked the West in the mystery that by 1900 had been extinguished by the bright light of day and the transformative change brought about by the winning of the West that he had so persistently championed. The modern West was mundane, virtually indistinguishable from the rest of America. Nocturnes restored tension and romance—excitement and danger. Night scenes whisked the viewer from the present to the past, where Remington's magic could cast its spell and imagination could roam free. He was now happy to say that those who wanted to see his pictures as literal renditions of what he had experienced were deluded or at least under his spell. In his diary he relished a visit to his studio by enthralled viewers who, looking at a painting, wanted to know what happened next—boys with ardent imaginations, he chortled, who did not recognize that he was a puppet master and his figures were marionettes dancing to his tune.[15]

Remington's nocturnes also represent a psychological shift. After Cuba, war no longer seemed a heroic contest between equals on a level field. Instead, in his scenario of the winning of the West, the Indians could now be portrayed as victims of circumstance. Was Frederic Remington a changed man? Had he recanted entirely his celebration of the winning of the West? In fact, Remington returned to his signature themes till the very end. A nocturne like *Fired On* (1907) had its precursor in action scenes from the past and could still be rendered in broad daylight in an oil like *Among the Led Horses*

"Among the Led Horses," 1909. *Sid Richardson Museum, Fort Worth, Tex.*

(1909). He still loved dramatic cavalry charges, and pictures showing the frontier army in action remain a fundamental part of Remington's legacy. We can still wallow in the power of his imagery in a painting like *The Fight for the Waterhole* (1901), a variation on the desperate stand that influenced John Ford's concluding battle scene in *Fort Apache* (1948), a story loosely based on Custer's Last Stand. In the aftermath, a surviving officer who knows the truth about the folly that precipitated disaster gazes at a heroic painting of the battle and, when questioned as to its veracity, replies, "Correct in every detail." Remington's art must be understood from that officer's perspective. Remington was, indeed, a very good friend to the army. His art may not be history exactly, but as a character in another John Ford western observes, "This is the West . . . When the legend becomes fact, print the legend." For Remington, the formulation was more personal: When *you* have made the legend fact, paint the legend.[16]

NOTES

1. Nelson A. Miles to Department and Post Commander, 31 Dec. 1895, in Allen Splete and Marilyn D. Splete, eds., *Frederic Remington—Selected Letters* (New York: Abbeville Press, 1988), p. 198; Peggy Samuels and Harold Samuels, *Frederic Remington: A Biography* (Garden City, N.Y.: Doubleday and Company, 1982), p. 211 (quotation in both). This essay reflects my understanding of Frederic Remington in 1997 when I delivered my talk at the Fort Robinson Conference that April. I subsequently did intensive work in Remington manuscripts in preparation for my catalog *The Frederic Remington Art Museum Collection* (Ogdensburg, N.Y.: Frederic Remington Art Museum, 2001), though nothing I encountered materially altered my understanding of Remington's relationship with the army. I did not deliver this talk again, but parts of it may echo my other published writings on Remington dating back to 1975. Important works on Remington that postdate 1997 include Emily Ballew Neff, with Wynne H. Phelan, *Frederic Remington: The Hogg Brothers Collection of the Museum of Fine Arts, Houston* (Princeton, N.J.: Princeton University Press in association with the Museum of Fine Arts, Houston, 2000); Nancy K. Anderson, with William C. Sharpe and Alexander Nemerov, *Frederic Remington: The Color of Night* (Washington, D.C.: National Gallery of Art, with Princeton University Press, Princeton, N.J., 2003); and Peter H. Hassrick, ed., *Frederic Remington: A Catalogue Raisonné II* (Norman: University of Oklahoma Press, in cooperation with the Buffalo Bill Center of the West, Cody, Wyo., 2016), an update of Hassrick and Melissa J. Webster's indispensable *Frederic Remington: A Catalogue Raisonne of Paintings, Watercolors and Drawings* (Cody, Wyo.: Buffalo Bill Historical Center, in association with University of Washington Press, Seattle, 1996). I can't conclude without acknowledging my friend Tom Buecker, who arranged for my participation in the Fort Robinson Conference in 1997 and again in 2013. I ended my Remington talk with remarks that I would like to repeat here: "I am grateful to Tom Buecker, who has put me up in the very fort Remington visited in 1905, in the very room Remington occupied, I like to think, and, I am certain, in the very cot Remington slept on. I'm not complaining, but he never was a lightweight. Thanks, Tom!"

2. *Personal Recollections and Observations of General Nelson A. Miles* . . . (Chicago: Werner Co., 1896), title page (first quotation); Miles to Department and Post Commander, 31 Dec. 1895 (second quotation); Owen Wister, "Introduction," in *Done in the Open: Drawings by Frederic Remington* (New York: P. F. Collier and Son, 1902), no pagination (third quotation). In a letter of 25 June 1895 (Frederic Remington Art Museum Archives, Ogdensburg, N.Y.), Miles wooed the artist by complimenting his article about their hunt together in New Mexico in 1893, "Bear-Chasing in the Rocky Mountains," *Harper's Monthly* 91 (July 1895): 240–51. Praising Remington's "descriptive powers," Miles added: "I think you will in time de-

velope as much skill with the pen as you have genius with the brush. . . . I want to talk with you about the possibility of your illustrating one or two old-time Indian scenes." Remington had long since learned the quid pro quo: pictures were proper payment for the special favors accorded him by the army. When he was notified of his election as an honorary member of the Officer's Club at Fort Grant, Arizona Territory, in April 1893, he reciprocated with the gift of an oil painting, *Revolution in Northern Mexico—Marching Regulars to the Front.* This prompted a resolution of thanks on 11 September 1894 declaring that Remington, "more than any other living civilian, has, by his art and kind sympathy, brought the United States Army to the favorable notice of the citizens of our Country" (Frederic Remington Art Museum Archives, Ogdensburg, N.Y.).

3. Deoch Fulton, ed., *The Journal of Lieut. Sydenham 1889, 1890; and His Notes on Frederic Remington* (New York: Public Library, 1940), p. 26.

4. William A. Coffin, "American Illustration of To-day (Third Paper)," *Scribner's* 11 (Mar. 1892): 348.

5. Frederic Remington, "A Scout with the Buffalo-Soldiers," *Century* 37 (Apr. 1889): 899–912. *Arrival of a Courie*r earned Remington election as an associate of the National Academy of Design. *See Frederic Remington 1861–1909: Paintings, Drawings and Sculpture* (Shreveport, La.: R. W. Norton Art Gallery, 1979), p. 32.

6. Frederic Remington to Powhatan Clarke, 25 Mar. 1890, in Splete and Splete, *Frederic Remington—Selected Letters*, p. 92.

7. A. R. Waud, *Custer's Last Fight*, in Frederick Whittaker, *A Complete Life of Gen. George A. Custer* (New York: Sheldon and Company, 1876), facing p. 606; and Frederic Remington, *The Last Stand*, in *Harper's Weekly* 35 (10 Jan. 1891): 24–25 (quotation from the accompanying editorial note on p. 107). For Remington's boyhood sketch *Custer's Last Fight, see Frederic Remington 1861–1909: Paintings, Drawings and Sculpture*, p. 49.

8. Frederic Remington to Powhatan Clarke, 20 June [1891], in Splete and Splete, *Frederic Remington—Selected Letters*, p. 19 (Remington quotations); Frederic Remington, "Cracker Cowboys of Florida," *Harper's Monthly* 91 (Aug. 1895): 339; and C. M. Fairbanks, "Artist Remington at Home and Afield," *Metropolitan Magazine* 4 (July 1896): 450 (quotation).

9. Perriton Maxwell, "Frederic Remington—Most Typical of American Artists," *Pearson's* 18 (Oct. 1907): 399.

10. For Remington's reworking of material, *see* Brian W. Dippie, "Frederic Remington's West: Where History Meets Myth," in Chris Bruce et al., *Myth of the West* (New York: Rizzoli, for the Henry Art Gallery, University of Washington, Seattle, 1990), pp. 111–19.

11. Frederic Remington to John Howard, 21 Jan. [1909], in Splete and Splete, *Frederic Remington—Selected Letters*, p. 419.

12. "Finds Flaws in Custer's Demand," *New York Herald*, 28 Apr. 1903; and Frederic Remington to Mary Fanton Roberts, 11 Dec. 1908, Mary Fanton Roberts Papers, Archives of American Art, Smithsonian Institution, Washington, D.C., Roll D163, (quotations). For the Remington-Schreyvogel dust up and Remington's efforts to escape the burden of his reputation ("But you and your art are one," a reporter told him), *see* Dippie, *The Frederic Remington Art Museum Collection*, pp. 218–20 and p. 23.

13. Frederic Remington to Poultney Bigelow, 9 Aug. 1897, in Splete and Splete, *Frederic Remington—Selected Letters*, p. 285 (first quotation); Remington to Owen Wister [June 1898], ibid., p. 224 (second quotation); Remington, "A Scout with the Buffalo-Soldiers," p. 912 (third quotation); *see* Frederic Remington, "With the Fifth Corps," *Harper's Monthly* 97 (Nov. 1898): 975, for his visceral reaction to what he encountered in Cuba at "the rear of a battle": "All the broken spirits, bloody bodies, hopeless, helpless suffering . . . so much more appalling than anything else in the world that words won't mean anything to one who has not seen it."

14. Frederic Remington to Owen Wister, 1 Sept. 1899, in Splete and Splete, *Frederic Remington—Selected Letters*, p. 233 (first quotation); Maxwell, "Frederic Remington—Most Typical of American Artists," pp. 404–5 (second quotation); and Remington to Powhatan Clarke, 30 Jan. 1890, in Splete and Splete, *Frederic Remington—Selected Letters*, p. 90 (third quotation).

15. Edwin Wildman, "Frederic Remington, the Man," *Outing* 41 (Mar. 1903): 715 (quotation); and Remington Diary 1907, entry for 10 July, Frederic Remington Art Museum Archives.

16. Quotations from *Fort Apache* (1948) and *The Man Who Shot Liberty Valance* (1962); *see* Brian W. Dippie, *Remington & Russell: The Sid Richardson Collection* (1985; revised ed., Austin: University of Texas Press, 1994), pp. 58–59.

6 : Lakota Perspectives on Wounded Knee, 1890

JEROME A. GREENE

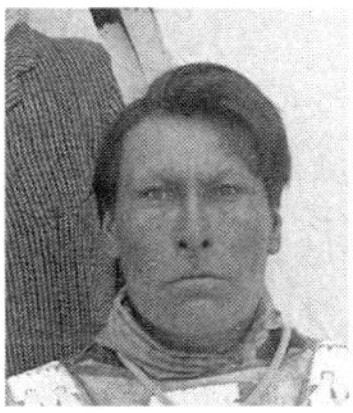

The Wounded Knee Massacre of 29 December 1890 resulted from an accumulation of adverse conditions, circumstances, and grievances among the Lakota Sioux following their wars with the United States government in the 1860s and 1870s. During their early reservation experience between 1868 and 1889, they faced reduction of their tribal land base in present North and South Dakota as well as prolonged societal stresses as the federal government manipulated them with land transactions that fostered their suspicion and continued unrest. In the late 1880s and early 1890s, the onset of crippling drought conditions and the appearance of epidemics of sickness were followed by government reduction of the Indians' beef allowance, compounding the people's sense of devastation. Many Lakotas turned to the Ghost Dance, a rite by which they sought transcendental deliverance from white oppression, reversion to their old ways, and spiritual reunion with long-dead ancestors. In response, the War Department sent troops onto the reservations to thwart disturbances anticipated by white settlers. The subsequent killing of the Hunkpapa Sioux spiritual leader Sitting Bull by Indian policemen at Standing Rock Indian Reservation compounded matters, driving some of the medicine man's followers to join Chief Big Foot's Miniconjou people as they fled south from the Cheyenne River Indian Reservation seeking refuge among Chief Red Cloud's people near Pine Ridge Agency.[1]

On 28 December a battalion of Seventh Cavalry troops under Major Samuel M. Whitside halted Big Foot's followers near Porcupine Butte on the Pine Ridge Indian Reservation and ushered them to nearby Wounded Knee Creek, approximately eighteen miles northeast of the agency. That night, more soldiers arrived—another battalion of the Seventh Cavalry, along with Battery E of the First Artillery with Hotchkiss guns, all under Colonel James W. Forsyth of the Seventh, who assumed command. The next morning, 29 December, efforts to disarm the warriors grew tense as armed units of cavalrymen surrounded the council circle. At about 9:15 A.M., as soldiers attempted to wrestle a gun from a warrior's grasp, shots suddenly erupted. Big Foot was one of the first to die in the gunfire. Over the course of several minutes, fifty-eight of Forsyth's soldiers fell killed or wounded as the warriors forced their way through a cordon of troops into a broad, deep ravine at the far side of Big Foot's camp. Soldiers fired after them, killing and wounding many men, women, and children in an unrestrained massacre before leaving the field to distant artillerymen. Those soldiers directed canister and exploding shell from four Hotchkiss guns situated on the brow of a low hill to the north, raking the camp and the nearby ravine where the people sought cover. The heavy shooting probably lasted close to an hour, although sporadic gunfire continued until late afternoon. The toll among Big Foot's Lakotas was at least 146 and perhaps more than 200 dead, many of them noncombatants, together with many wounded. Forsyth returned to Pine Ridge Agency that night with the army casualties along with many of Big Foot's followers who had been injured.[2]

Much of what happened to them during the eruption at Wounded Knee remained with the Lakotas through succeeding decades as well as generations. All people have impressions about events that have shaped them, and the Lakotas are no exception. Lakota testimony about the grim events of 29 December 1890—both immediate and reminiscent statements—constitutes an important body of information. These personal insights have remained crucial for those who survived and for the relatives, friends, and others of those who did not. Taken together, the accounts show how deadly the action became as it quickly intensified from a seeming initial shooting by warriors into a defensive reaction by troops before climaxing in an unchecked and devastating slaughter of innocents. One hesitates to use the term "bloodlust" to explain what happened at Wounded Knee, but the term is a clear reflection of how the events must have seemed to the Indians involved, particularly noncombatant women, children, and elderly men.

Unlike their predecessors of the 1860s and 1870s in the wilds of early Dakota, Wyoming, and Montana, many in the Lakota generation who experienced Wounded Knee had known reservation life for more than two decades. Through education and day-to-day contact with whites, they had become increasingly conversant in English over time. Moreover, because of their closer physical proximity to whites, Lakota statements were sought out and recorded. Thus, Lakota survivor accounts have been gathered and accumulated since the time of the events at Wounded Knee, with their volume and content becoming ever richer. Taken together, they provide clear images of what happened from individual points of view. Redundancy of detail in these testimonies demonstrates honesty and tends to validate accuracy. Drawing on these valuable resources, the following composite narrative based on Lakota reminiscences attempts to tell the story from their perspective.[3]

After they arrived with Whitside's soldiers at Wounded Knee Creek (Canke Opi Wahkpala) on the night of 28 December, the people grew tense. They became especially anxious when the troops placed a chain of sentinels around them. Thirteen-year-old Alice Ghost Horse, from Cheyenne River, recalled: "My mother and I went down to the creek to go to the bathroom and pick up some sticks for the fire but two soldiers were following us around and they appeared to be drunk. They were saying bad words to us.... Some of the young men were detailed to watch the soldier guards all night." Many did not sleep, and among some there was a sense of foreboding. "All night long the soldiers had lights [lanterns] and were working at something," remembered young Paul High Back. "We could hear the noise and rattle of iron being moved around and it made us all very nervous." Lakota survivors recalled one or more Indian criers announcing the council of men to meet with Colonel Forsyth and telling the women to ready the wagons to start for the agency.[4] They recalled hearing Forsyth and some of the officers asking for the Indians' guns and seeing interpreters John Shangrau and Philip Wells in the circle translating the proceedings.

After being requested to return to the camp and bring back their guns to turn in at the council, some of the men complied and deposited twenty-five of the arms in a pile near the front of the assembly area. But the officer in charge (either Forsyth or Major Whitside) demanded more. Big Foot had responded that there were no more guns, but the officer told him that he would have to search the camp. The ailing chief concurred. According to the Miniconjou Joseph Horn Cloud, then sixteen years old, the soldiers went to the camp and "took sacks out of wagons and emptied them on the ground." They went into tents, he said, "and everywhere [else] examining, picked up some old shotguns, knives, tomahawks, arrows and awls; and they searched the persons of the women." Alice Ghost Horse said of the search: "They were really rude about it, they scattered our belongings all over the ground." A Miniconjou named Long Bull insisted: "We did not want to fight. The soldiers said we must give up our guns and some of us did. I had no gun. Then the soldiers went into the tepees and kicked the beds about and upset everything a great deal. Some Indians had guns under their blankets [at the assembly], hiding them, for an Indian thinks much of his gun. The soldiers used the Indians very roughly and made them mad, until by and by 'Sits Straight' (the medicine man) gave the signal to shoot."[5]

At length, the officer called for disarming the men in the council, saying, as Horn Cloud recalled, "I want the same number of soldiers to stand in front of the Indians and take their cartridges out of their guns and cock them and aim at their foreheads and pull the triggers. After this you will be free." Following this confusing statement, he told them they would then proceed to Pine Ridge Agency. The threatening actions and talk stressed the men, some of whom urged the others to be courageous. Big Foot called for calm, telling the men to do nothing to make the situation worse. He was so sick that he could not sit erect and had to lie down on the ground repeatedly. Horn Cloud said that Captain Wallace told him to alert the women to saddle their horses and move the wagons or else there would be trouble, because "that officer [presumably Forsyth] is half shot [drunk]." A medicine man moved around the council area, waving his arms and singing Ghost Dance songs. Indians and troops alike reported another man moving about, singing the same songs.[6]

Following the main search of the camp, the soldiers had begun moving around the council area taking guns from individuals. Horn Cloud and his thirty-two-year-old brother, Iron Hail (also known as

Dewey Beard, Beard, and Dewey Horn Cloud), said that a young deaf man named Black Coyote (sometimes called Black Fox) held his gun over his head with both hands. Horn Cloud said he was complaining that the gun "had cost him a good deal of money, that if anybody wanted it he must pay for it, for he would not give it up without pay." Two sergeants grabbed his arms, while a third wrestled the gun from him. "Just as the struggle between him and the sergeants began," Horn Cloud remembered, "someone cried: 'Look out! Look out!' These words were scarcely uttered when the gun went off elevated in the air at an angle of about 45 degrees." Instantly, he said, "there was a volley from the soldiers standing around the circle. These shot the men in the back." When the shooting started, Horn Cloud said, "the women ran to the ravine. The shooting was in every direction. Soldiers shot into one another. Many Indians in the circle were killed. Many of them mingled with the soldiers behind them, picking up guns from dead soldiers and taking cartridge belts. They took guns they had turned over and the cartridge belts that they had turned over with them."[7]

Iron Hail protested that the young man had intended to put his gun down and had not pointed the weapon at anyone. But "all the soldiers standing around fired at once, just like one gun," and then "everybody was rolling and kicking on the ground," he said, adding that "the soldiers were firing on the Indians & stepping backwards & firing." In the quickly diffusing smoky haze it became impossible to see anybody or anything. "There was no wind to clear it away," Horn Cloud said. "It hung like a pall over the field. Through rifts in the smoke heads and feet would be visible. Women were killed in the beginning of the fight just the same as the men were killed."[8]

In an account taken within days of Wounded Knee, a brother of Big Foot named Frog was among those hospitalized for injuries received in the melee. He was at the assembly, he said, seated near the front of the Miniconjou leader's tent. "Then a lot of soldiers got in between us . . . (men) and our camp, separating us (men) from the women and children." Frog and the older men turned over their guns on request. "I saw an Indian with a gun under his blanket and the soldiers saw it at the same time, and they took it away from him," he said. Frog listened to the medicine man's incantations, then pulled his blanket over his head until he heard loud talking. "I uncovered my head, and saw everyone had arisen on his feet, and I heard a shot coming from where the young Indians stood. Shortly after that I was shot down, and I laid there as I fell. The firing was so fast and the smoke and dust so thick I did not see much more of the fight until it was over." Frog then heard Philip Wells speaking to those on the ground.[9]

Similarly, an Oglala named Help Them, who had traveled from Cheyenne River with Big Foot's people, told how the medicine man had been performing Ghost Dance maneuvers:

> He stopped, turned around facing a crowd of young Indians (who were standing together with their guns concealed under their blankets) and spoke to them, but I could not hear what they said, though I heard them all answer "How." Shortly after I heard a white man saying something in excited tones, which I could not understand, and . . . I saw some of the Indians throw off their blankets and raise their guns, [and] one of the Indians fired a shot. . . . As I turned around, I heard a few shots following the first. Then the firing began so fast, I could not tell what happened after that.[10]

Another early statement by Hehakawanyakapi (Elks Saw Him) reported much the same. He had surrendered his Winchester. As a soldier was taking bullets from his cartridge belt, a gunshot sounded. He watched a warrior throw off his sheet blanket. When the general shooting started, Hehakawanyakapi hit the ground. When he sprang up to run, bullets struck him in both legs. Like other wounded Indians, he was later treated in the makeshift ward in the Episcopal church at Pine Ridge.[11]

Private Spotted Horse, an army scout who witnessed the beginning of the encounter, said that the first shot came from a young man and killed an army officer. "As soon as this shot was fired, the Indians immediately began drawing their knives and they were exhorted from all sides to desist, but this was not obeyed. Consequently, the firing began immediately on the part of the soldiers." Similarly, Sergeant John Ghost Bear, also of the Indian scouts, stated that during the disarmament Captain George D. Wallace "stepped over to an

Indian named Slippery Skin, who was not in line, and Slippery Skin shot and killed . . . Wallace. That started the fight, and the Indians started to run, most of them up the large draw [ravine], just south of where the Indians were being disarmed." In the account he gave to the Oglala warrior Black Elk, Dog Chief told of the disarmament of two armed Indians (one of them also named Yellow Bird) who wore white sheets in the council with only their eyes showing. When an officer attempted to take Yellow Bird's rifle, the two men ended up wrestling on the ground. The gun went off. "This fellow did not want to give up his gun, and did not intend to shoot the white man at all—the gun just went off." In the fighting that followed, Dog Chief said, Yellow Bird managed to occupy an army tent and shot several soldiers before he was himself killed and the tent burned.[12]

High Back maintained that before the shooting began two Indians with guns were targeted by cavalry troopers who advanced to take their weapons. "Suddenly," he reported, "all the rest of the soldiers raised their guns and fired right into us." According to Miniconjou Andrew Good Thunder, when it was reported to Big Foot that Black Coyote had started acting up, telling the men with guns to discard their blankets, Big Foot "said not to do what Black Coyote advised, as [Big Foot] expected to locate there [meaning at Pine Ridge] & didn't want any trouble." When this was repeated to Black Coyote, he threw his blanket aside "& put a cartridge into his gun & two soldiers began back up begging him to put his gun down." Good Thunder said Black Coyote then "shot one of the soldiers who was backing up. I saw this." Good Thunder also recalled seeing Father Francis M. Craft "in the midst of us with both hands up saying something but I did not hear what. . . . We had tried to avoid trouble but it seemed that through Black Coyote's disobedience . . . we got right into the middle of it. I was wounded in several places. My own sister was killed there. Three of my nephews were killed there. . . . I managed to run to a coulee & some of us fought our way and escaped."[13]

A mixed-blood Oglala named Zella Vespucia had carried mail from the agency to Whitside's command the previous day. As a witness to the disarmament, he said that when the proposal was finally made to search the men in the assembly, "there were about twenty-one on one side who gave up their guns very peacefully":

> When the soldiers stepped over to the next gang and began to disarm them there was a young man by the name of His Dog who had a gun and objected to give it up. He had been quite intimate with the medicine man. When His Dog refused to give up [his gun] he fired a shot. Then all of the rest of the Indians fired a volley before the soldiers did anything. Then some of them said, "Look out!," several times. Then one buck with a painted ghost shirt on shot and Capt. Wallace staggered back. By that time an Indian came up behind him, and taking from his hand a war club . . . struck him several blows on the cranium until he fell dead on the ground. . . . I don't say that from hearsay, but I was in the center of the fight without any arms to fight with, except a belt full of cartridges. . . . When they killed Capt. Wallace they did not cease shooting, but became all the worse. I heard a man, who after the battle I found out was Lieut. Nicholson, say two or three times: "Don't shoot squaws," and after that several others repeated the same words.[14]

In one of the most comprehensive of the Indian statements, Horn Cloud said of the initial shooting: "It was just like a hail-storm with shots in all directions." In the confusion, "all we thought about . . . was to get away," said Paul High Back. "The morning was cloudy and damp and the smoke from the guns did not rise but settled right on us. From then on nothing could be seen very plain. The soldiers were rushing around shooting all of us that they could see to shoot." He was hit in the hand as he dashed blindly through the cloud. In the combat Iron Hail, armed with only a knife, sought to get a gun and rushed a soldier so closely that the man fired his carbine right next to Iron Hail's ear, momentarily deafening him. In the rising smoke the Indian yanked the gun away, stabbing the man, who grabbed him by the throat. Iron Hail knifed the man repeatedly until he died. He then took the gun and sprinted toward the ravine behind the camp. He was wounded before he got there, however, an injury that severely debilitated his right arm. He finally shot a soldier but received a flesh wound in the leg as he entered the gulch.[15]

Others who broke through the soldiers raced with the women and children into the ravine and then ran in either direction. Iron Hail encountered soldiers and other fleeing Lakotas several times as he headed west up the dry wash where he ultimately witnessed his own

Map of Lakotas' paths while fleeing from the Wounded Knee Massacre, drawn by Robert G. Pilk. Greene, *American Carnage* (Norman: University of Oklahoma Press, 2014)

mother killed. "Soldiers on both sides of the ravine shot at her and killed her." He saw "lots of women and children lying along the ravine, some alive and some dead." Iron Hail told some young men to "take courage and do all they could to defend the women," but "an awful fire was concentrated on them now and nothing could be seen for the smoke. In the bottom of the ravine the bullets raised more dust than there was smoke, so that they could not see one another." Horn Cloud recalled that some women with babies excavated hollows inside the ravine in which to hide them. Mothers and infants were killed together. "One mother lay dead," he said, "her breast covered with blood from her wound, and her little child was standing by her and nursing."[16]

Lakota survivor accounts of the furious action inside the council area are scarce. Many if not most of the Sioux men present were killed in the circle. Only the warriors who broke through the soldier cordon at the breach between Troops K and B who lived or already lay wounded on the field were able to describe how the fighting began. Beyond the thunderous explosion of the initial firing, which many of the people in the area of the Sioux camp clearly recalled hearing, most other survivor accounts described the action as it gravitated to the big ravine and beyond, where soldier targeting of noncombatants intensified. The scout Ghost Bear recalled that "a few of the Indian men picked up the guns of the soldiers that had been killed, and used them to fight the soldiers; but most of them had nothing to fight with."[17]

Alice Ghost Horse remembered the cavalrymen "shooting at every Lakota who was running and it didn't matter if you were a child or woman. They shot you anyway. . . . We fled into the ravines where the plum bushes were the thickest and dived in like frightened rabbits. The gunfire was pretty heavy and people were hollering for their children and children were crying everywhere." Her father went back to help the others but soon returned wounded in a leg. He took Alice's young brother and moved down the ravine, telling Alice and her mother that he would return for them. "Soon afterwards my father came crawling back . . . and said 'they killed my son' and started to cry so we cried a little bit. . . . My father said we should move to a better hiding place but my mother objected again, saying we should all die here together. She told me to stand up so I did but my father pulled me down."[18]

They crawled to a deeper part of the ravine, then Alice's father left again to help others. More people took shelter in the ravine. "Four of them died right there, but there was nothing anybody could do." One man who arrived "told us that my father was killed instantly. We all cried for a little bit because the soldiers were still firing their rifles at anything that moved." Alice and her mother remained hidden in the brush in the deep recesses of the ravine until late afternoon when the sounds of gunfire slackened. The wounded High Back also made it to the ravine, where he sought safety by crawling beneath the bodies of other casualties. But he still took more bullets. Peter One Skunk, who was struck in the head by a bullet during the soldiers' opening volley, also made his way to the ravine and hid. He eventually caught a horse and broke free from the turmoil. When his horse was killed shortly afterward, One Skunk played dead and was left alone by the troops. In time, he caught another horse and got away.[19]

Elsewhere, as the action continued, some of those who headed west in the ravine found protection in the acre-sized gulch area known as "the pocket," including Horn Cloud, several of his brothers, and several cousins, along with two old men, a woman named Helena Long Bull, and her small son. One brother, William Horn Cloud, was killed in the pocket. Several more received wounds there, and one named White Lance was badly injured but subsequently recovered. Iron Hail said that he killed at least five soldiers while in the pocket. When the soldiers brought a Hotchkiss gun forward to fire directly at these people, he said, it became "a storm of thunder and hail." "There went up from these dying people," he said,

> a medley of death songs that would make the hardest heart weep. . . . The death song is expressive of their wish to die. . . . It expresses that the singer is anxious to die, too. At this time I am unable to do anything more, and I took a rest, telling my brothers to keep up courage. The cannon were pouring in their shots and breaking down the banks which were giving protection. . . . The soldiers were pretty close to the edge of the bank and these kept up a continual fire. . . . Even if there was no more shooting, the smoke was so thick that the wounded could not live for it; it was suffocating. The Hotchkiss had been shooting rapidly and one Indian had got killed by it. His body was penetrated in the pit of the stomach by a Hotchkiss shell, which tore a hole through his body six inches in diameter. The man was insensible, but breathed for an hour when he expired. At the same time this man was shot, a young woman . . . was shot through between the shoulders. . . . [I] heard a laugh and looked at her and she was smiling, all unconscious that she was wounded. The next moment a young man was shot down right in front this woman. When the man fell, his bow and arrows fell all around on the ground.[20]

Horn Cloud moved fluidly through the area and collected numerous horses that he distributed to others to aid their escape. He continued fighting troops to the west and overhearing the arrival of the Pine Ridge Indians, who managed to see the prisoners captured from the pocket and took some of them back to the agency. Several captives raced back to the ravine, where soldiers killed three of them. Iron Hail also encountered several of the Pine Ridge Oglalas on horses and went with them, soon meeting his brother Horn Cloud, who told him that his father was also dead. Of eleven family members at Wounded Knee, Horn Cloud and Iron Hail lost their mother (Yellow Leaf) and father (a headman named Horned Cloud); and two brothers (Sherman and William). Iron Hail lost his wife (Wears Eagle, also known as White Face), killed at the scene, and would lose his infant son, Wet Feet, who within a short time would die from illness contracted during the massacre. Iron Hail's cousin, Pretty Enemy, who lived with the family, also died there. Iron Hail suffered two wounds in the fighting, while another brother, Daniel Horn Cloud, received four wounds. Iron Hail and Horn Cloud proceeded west from the upheaval at Wounded Knee to a point near the mission and then headed north to join other Indians along White Clay Creek as they withdrew from the agency area. When they arrived, those people "were crying and singing death songs" and shook hands with them. As night descended at Wounded Knee, small knots of surviving Lakotas made their way north through draws and creek bottoms in the gathering chill.[21]

Other Lakotas present that day offered their own observations. A man named White Lance (no relation to Horn Cloud and Iron Hail) also told of the gathering of the men and the pile of surrendered guns that accrued near the center of the assembly:

> It was understood that just as soon as all the guns were stacked in the center we were to continue on the Pine Ridge Agency. Big Foot was placed right in the doorway of the tent and I stood right to his left side. I could see that there was a commotion among the soldiers and I saw on looking back they had their guns in position ready to fire. There were two officers in the center; the one that was standing to the left gave a command in a loud voice, then [after the initial outburst of shooting] we couldn't see anything for [the] smoke. The smoke was so dense I couldn't see anything so I didn't make a move, just stood there. When it cleared up a little . . .

Daniel Horn Cloud (White Lance), Joseph Horn Cloud, and
Dewey Beard (Iron Hail), 1907. *Nebraska State Historical Society*

> I saw Big Foot lying down with blood on his forehead and his head to the right side. . . . I went a little ways then. I was knocked down. I was unconscious for a little while. I was shot then and wounded and I went to this little wide cut bank [the ravine?] and there I found that we were surrounded by soldiers. Some [of us were] already wounded, some dead, but [they] continued to fire on us. . . . I stayed there all day with these young fellows, boys then, and since then I have been unable to use my left arm but I struggled along.[22]

When the shooting started at the council ground, twelve-year-old James Pipe on Head had just delivered tobacco to Big Foot, his ailing grandfather, who was prostrate in the center of the circle. The old chief had just told the boy to return to his grandmother in the camp. At the eruption of firing, "I started to run towards the hillside [on the west]," Pipe on Head said. "I came across a little boy. I took the little boy by the hand and all at once someone came on the side of me and took hold of my hand. This woman was my mother. She had a baby on her back, my sister, but this girl that she was carrying . . . was shot. While we were running we saw on the ground dust flying [and] some of the bullets struck near us." But James and his mother managed to escape and survived.[23]

Rough Feather, who was about twenty-two at Wounded Knee, remembered looking back and seeing the soldiers aiming their guns at the men in the assembly. "It sounded much the sound of tearing canvass [*sic*], when they fired," he said. "As I heard the crash I became unconscious. Something struck me. As I was standing there I happened to look up and the smoke was awfully dense, but I could now make out a face right in front of me." Rough Feather followed the man, who soon engaged a soldier hand-to-hand as the Indian tried to bolt through the troops to reach the ravine. Another soldier struck Rough Feather in the chest with his carbine, painfully hurting him, but the warrior broke through toward the ravine before a man named Ghost Bear (the scout?) urged him to lie down on the flat where many of the men as well as women had fallen. After the firing ceased, Rough Feather heard Philip Wells, the interpreter known as the Fox, speak to those on the ground: "All of you that are still alive get up and come on over, you will not be molested or shot at any more." Yet fearful, Rough Feather lay still until Wells repeated the directive. Then he got up and helped load a wagon with wounded from the scene, including one that he believed was the wife of Big Foot.[24]

Another survivor was Medicine Woman, a Lakota also known as Mrs. Mousseau, who was in the camp when the soldiers ransacked it looking for guns and other weapons. When the shooting broke out, "the smoke was awful thick," she recalled.[25] "I was wounded at the first fire, but I was so scared I did not feel it. My husband was killed there and my little girl, and a little boy baby on my back was [also] killed by a bullet which also broke my elbow, so that I dropped the body." As she and her mother sought to escape, they carried a dead child with them. All of this occurred as they fled through the camp toward the ravine. "The soldiers followed us up and kept firing," she said. She and her mother ascended the dry ravine but eventually turned back and returned to Wounded Knee Creek and moved downstream. They spent the night in a snowstorm before taking shelter for two days in a shack. "We didn't have anything to eat or drink and we were found in that condition by the Indian Scouts and were taken to the Agency."[26]

A youth named Edward Owl King, like so many others, fled west up the ravine after the shooting started. "There were some ponies, women and children shot down and scattered, and while running I stepped on them." He gained the pocket and said "it wasn't a very deep place, and that was where many of the Indians were shot and killed. I was shot too, but did not die." Owl King reported that a soldier pulled him out of the pocket. But when he and others began ascending a hill, troops again fired at him. Another Indian rescued him, taking him into a deep recess where he remained until dark. "I was a boy, my sister and mother were killed. I was the only survivor of the family."[27]

Other women participants included Nellie Knife and Mrs. Rough Feather. Nellie Knife was packing that morning while the men attended the council. "All at once I heard an awful noise. As the shots were fired the women and children ran for a safe place to hide. I ran toward the flat and as I ran I saw many people were already killed. I was running with a young girl named Brown Ear Horse, but she got shot so I went on and left her." She passed the wife of One Skunk, who was also wounded and screaming. "I could not help her as the bullets were flying thick and I wanted to get to a safe place. . . . After the firing stopped . . . I returned to see if I could find any of my people. My mother-in-law, my sister-in-law and many brothers were dead.... My father-in-law, Little Bull, was alive but his leg was broken."[28] Likewise, after the gunfire opened Mrs. Rough Feather saw "nearly all the people on the ground bleeding." In sheer terror, she ran for safety with the others to the ravine south of the camp, following them up the gulch while "bullets flew all around us.... I was not hit one time, [but] my father, my mother, my grandmother, my older brother and my younger brother were all killed. My son who was two years old was shot in the mouth [and] that later caused his death."[29]

When young Henry Jackson heard the initial crash of guns, he and his mother had just been loading a wagon in the camp. They started running when a bullet hit her in the head, killing her instantly. Henry's sister, running ahead, came back for him, and they started into the large ravine that was filling with fleeing people and moved up the gulch with the crowd until they were helped out. "I have never said anything about this," said Henry. "I didn't like to on account of my mother who was shot right with me and it appears that it just happened this morning [ca. 1936–37]; it makes me feel sad."[30]

Like so many others, John Little Finger, also known as Yellow Horn, rushed to reach protection in the big ravine. "When I reached the ravine . . . there was a lot of Indians following [west] up the ravine and I was with them, and on each side . . . soldiers were shooting down on us until we got so far we couldn't go any further, as a line of soldiers got in front of us." These people took refuge in the washout called the pocket, where the soldiers continued shooting at them until Indian scouts called to them to come out. Most of them then submitted. Little Finger, however, had been shot in the leg and foot and instead crawled some distance before emerging on a flat of land. He then spotted the mounted warriors from Pine Ridge Agency who had responded to the distant shooting. As the soldiers headed east, Little Finger got away with those Indians and was taken to the agency, away from the day's horror.[31]

Some participants provided focused data on one or more aspects of their time at Wounded Knee. Nearly all Lakota accounts allude to the density of smoke in the assembly area at the outbreak of shooting. Peter Stand remembered how unbearably incapacitating it became and how many of the Indians benefited from the concealing cloud. "As the volley was flying into us, we couldn't see anything—

everything was smoking from then on; this valley was just covered with smoke, so I didn't see anything. Right after the volley was fired, I heard somebody bellow in Indian for them to throw themselves flat on the ground, so I did as he announced." Stand soon afterward got lost in the smoke as he tried to orient himself to the camp. He ran into one person then another before reaching the camp and then the ravine, where he and others dug a trench. There he stayed for the duration of the shooting. After the soldiers left, he and other survivors started west up the ravine on foot. Many accounts cite the upper ravine as promising early shelter from the soldiers' guns as well as a means to get away from the opening turmoil and to potential hiding places. The ravine also served eventually as a lifeline to any help that might arrive from Pine Ridge, such as those warriors who managed to get away with the captured women and children.[32]

Charley Blue Arm said that the "cannons on the hill . . . were firing at the Indians that were trying to escape, and the bullets hit the dirt all around us and, of course, that made us run faster, for we knew that they were trying to kill all of us." He reached the ravine too and moved up it to a point "where the bullets could not reach us." Blue Arm said that the people lay concealed there "all day until the sun went down," and when the soldiers were gone "we went out to hunt for our people." He added: "We were all tired out and frightened and besides we were worried about our relatives."[33]

Elaine Goodale remembered that she and several teachers were preparing presents and candy bags for the children at the Episcopal church in Pine Ridge Agency that morning. A muted "distant thunder" abruptly "sent cold shivers down our backs," she said. "Within an incredibly short time came first reports of the slaughter at Wounded Knee. We were told, indeed, that the cavalry had been cut off from reaching us and that we were at the mercy of a maddened horde of Indians!"[34]

Among others at the agency who heard the muffled sound of discharging Hotchkiss guns was Black Elk. "I knew from the sound that it must be wagon-guns (cannon) going off." As the shooting persisted, he donned the ghost shirt that he had earlier fashioned, one with a flaming rainbow and red lightning streaks. He then painted his face red, placed an eagle feather in his hair, and started for Wounded Knee. He took no weapon, only his sacred bow, which made him impervious to bullets. As he rode from the agency, Black Elk drew a number of companions to him. After a while they reached a high ridge from which they saw in the distance the area with the ravine cutting the terrain rising in their direction. The Hotchkiss guns still blazed away, and troops could be seen posted about the high ground while others fired at the people in the gulch. Black Elk's party saw women with children—those who had emerged from the pocket—clustered under a bank with cavalry guarding them. Out of sight, the warriors sang a song of courage before charging directly toward the soldiers, who fired at them and fled. The warriors rescued the women and children and sent them to safety. Later Black Elk, in a measure of his bravery, by himself charged the soldiers, who fired many bullets at him. "I ran my horse right close to them, and then swung around. Some soldiers across the gulch began shooting at me too, but I got back to the others and was not hurt at all." He added: "I had to hold my bow in front of me in the air to be bullet-proof but just as I had gotten over the hill after completing my charge, I let my bow down and I could feel some bullets passing through my ghost dance shirt near my hip."[35]

Soon more Lakotas from the agency appeared, and together all the warriors charged the troops, who fell back along the high ground. As Black Elk recalled,

> We followed down the dry gulch. . . . Dead and wounded women and children and little babies were scattered all along there where they had been trying to run away. The soldiers had followed along the gulch, as they ran, and murdered them. . . . Sometimes they were in heaps because they had huddled together, and some were scattered along. Sometimes bunches of them had been killed and torn to pieces where the wagon guns hit them. . . . There were two little boys at one place in this gulch [the boys were actually about fifteen years old]. They had guns and they had been killing soldiers all by themselves. We could see the soldiers they had killed. The boys were all alone there and they were not hurt. These were very brave little boys.

After the army command pulled out with the dead and wounded soldiers and wounded Lakotas, Black Elk and the others returned to help and to survey the scene. "Men and women and children were heaped and scattered all over the flat at the bottom of the little hill where the soldiers had their wagon-guns, and westward up the dry gulch all the way to the high ridge, the dead women and children and babies were scattered." Black Elk, his heart heavy from what he had seen, returned to the vicinity of Pine Ridge Agency then followed down White Clay Creek to reach the Oglalas who had departed that day. He and a companion, Red Crow, brought with them two babies they had rescued at Wounded Knee.[36]

When it was finally over, and the cavalrymen with lumbering wagons and ambulances bearing casualties from Wounded Knee had started away, those Lakotas who were still alive and able to move picked themselves up and helped others off the field. Among them were Alice Ghost Horse and her mother, with High Back. They had hidden for hours under dense thickets in the bottom of the large dry ravine. Stepping around bodies of people and animals and listening to those weeping and crying for relatives and water, they found their way to Wounded Knee Creek and started north through the cold and uncertain night. High Back recalled finding several women and children, some of them wounded. The survivors agreed to split into three groups so that they would not all be found together if the soldiers came back. The party traveling with Alice Ghost Horse and her mother numbered about thirteen. On the morning of 30 December, the group paused on a hill to rest beneath wind-driven clouds now threatening a storm. Boys nearby spied approaching riders, which sent the people scrambling into coulees, but the riders proved to be Lakotas. On their arrival, they all shook hands and cried together. A woman offered dried meat to the riders, who had not eaten in over a day. They pressed on northwestwardly as wind and storm clouds graduated into a blizzard, forcing the group into a vacant cabin, where they built a fire and stayed warm through the night. The next day they advanced through blowing snow, making their way toward the secure and impervious highlands. Eventually, they came upon a mixed village of Brules and Oglalas that included the Ghost Dance stalwart Short Bull.

On the day of the massacre, Short Bull and his immediate followers were moving south up White Clay Creek on the trail of people who had preceded them in going in to the agency. His people, too, had heard the shooting of the Hotchkiss guns far to the east. As they caught up with the others near the Holy Rosary Mission, they learned the shocking news that Big Foot's band had been wiped out. Short Bull's own cousin, Many Wounds, who had fled the scene, appeared in Short Bull's village with a gunshot wound in his shoulder. After other Indians began withdrawing from the vicinity of the agency and the mission amid continuing reports of the slaughter, Short Bull and his followers rode the next morning to Wounded Knee and were among the first to inspect the site. Short Bull located an uncle who had been wounded, and his people collected forty injured survivors. They placed some in a vacant building, where other Lakotas retrieved them for medical help at the agency. Salvaging discarded farm wagons, Short Bull returned with the others to his camp, where Alice Ghost Horse and her party soon joined them. Those traveling with High Back also met some other Lakotas, who came out to see what was happening. "They were very angry and in a very hostile mood," Ghost Horse recalled. "They took care of us and took us over to their camp."[37]

Through their individual and family perspectives, Lakota accounts dramatically personalize the events at Wounded Knee. They impart important knowledge of how individuals and groups reacted, interacted, succumbed, and endured. They amplify and sometimes correct conclusions found in government documents. More than anything, they give strength and broader dimension and provide empathy about the entire affair. They describe all aspects of the experience, from the night of the Indians' arrival to the morning council and multiple searches for weapons, the outbreak of shooting, the killing on the plain and in the dry ravine, the opening of the Hotchkiss guns and the fighting in the pocket, the departure of soldiers from the field, the exodus of survivors, and the arrival of others not immediately involved. More than anything, they give context, emphasis, and depth to the story of Wounded Knee.

In his own research on Wounded Knee, the avocational historian Walter M. Camp, after lengthy interviews and correspondence with tribal participants, offered succinct thoughts about how the situation in the assembly area managed to evolve into a massacre. His conclusions afford something of a window into Lakota views of the event in the early twentieth century:

> The Ind[ians] say that, as a whole, they were not inclined to resist giving up guns. When the soldiers were disarming [them] just before firing began, it was the intention generally to give up the guns & they were doing so. There were, however, among them two discontented Ind[ian]s who kept up an agitation to resist, but they were told to keep still. Nevertheless those two kept declaring that they would not surrender their guns and they were very bitter to see that the rest were doing so, and they would not be made to keep still. One of them kept calling out in a loud voice (one whom the white men took for a medicine man) and throwing dirt on his shoulders. He had a gun cocked under his blanket and a knife, and when, at length, a soldier came up to search him, he drew his gun and shot the soldier through, and then began cutting with his knife. The fight then started generally. The two loud Ind[ian]s referred to were the cause of it. They blame the soldiers for wanton killing. The gatling gun [*sic*: Hotchkiss guns were] turned on the lodges, killing women and children, who were entirely innocent and knew nothing of what was taking place where the disarming was going on. As soon as the firing commenced they tried to get away and many were killed on the flat south of the battlefield while driving off in wagons. A squaw with a baby on her back was killed on the road to the agency 1¼ miles from the battlefield.[38]

Variances and vagaries among the Indian and army participant accounts be what they may, somewhere within them lies the truth of Wounded Knee. While the record left by the soldiers and their officers often has a bureaucratic slant, it is often legitimized by the personal tribal views. Within both sets of accounts, all aspects of what we know about Wounded Knee are exposed, from horrific beginning to tragic end. Discrepancies between army and Indian accounts mainly concern the outbreak of shooting in the assembly or council area. No known Lakota statements mention the throwing aside of blankets by armed warriors at the inception of the shooting—likely because the majority of warriors in the council area were killed by the soldiers in the outburst of gunfire. Many if not most Lakota recollections came from women and other noncombatants (many of them children at the time) who stood outside the council area, at the edge of the camp, or elsewhere behind the cordon of soldiers of the Seventh Cavalry.

Consequently, their firsthand perception of the action began with the shooting, ultimately toward and into the camp itself.

Of the 370 or so Lakota people arrested by Major Samuel M. Whitside east of Porcupine Creek and escorted to Wounded Knee, as many as 200 and perhaps more certainly died violently there or elsewhere from wounds received. (In addition, a large number apparently received wounds and survived.) Within days 146 bodies were gathered and hastily interred, while family members retrieved others for burial elsewhere after 29 December. Shortly thereafter, 14 more bodies (including those who succumbed from wounds at a makeshift hospital at the Episcopal church in Pine Ridge, where they were taken) boosted the total of positively known dead to 160. While an official army report the following February raised the likely number to 200, the final tally might indeed have been higher. Nor were all the dead Sioux on the site interred on 3–4 January. As late as 12 January, a Sixth Cavalry private at the scene beheld "old and young of both sexes that were not [yet] buried." Efforts to chronicle the names and exact number of fatalities have proceeded over the decades since. Yet, despite the figures given above and well-considered approximations, the precise number of Lakotas killed at Wounded Knee has been and remains impossible to determine. Whatever the total, the day's events had rendered Wounded Knee, as John Little Finger, a grandson of Big Foot, was to say, "the Place of the Big Killings."[39]

NOTES

1. For details of the conditions and sequential events preceding Wounded Knee, *see* Jerome A. Greene, *American Carnage: Wounded Knee, 1890* (Norman: University of Oklahoma Press, 2014), pp. 23–81, 167–90. For contemporary perspectives of events, *see* Charles H. Cressey, *Sting of the Bee: A Day-by-Day Account of Wounded Knee and the Sioux Outbreak of 1890–91 as Recorded in the Omaha Bee*, comp. Samuel L. Russell (Carlisle, Pa.: Russell Martial Research, 2016).

2. Greene, *American Carnage*, pp. 215–46.

3. For information on the status of education and English usage among Lakotas at Cheyenne River and Standing Rock in 1889 and 1890, *see* "Report of Cheyenne River Agency," 5 Aug. 1890 (pp. 42–44), and "Report of Standing Rock Agency," 26 Aug. 1890 (pp. 37–38), in *Report of the Commissioner of Indian Affairs, 1890* (Washington, D.C.: Government Printing Office, 1890); and "Report of Cheyenne Agency," 17 Aug. 1891, in *Report of the Commissioner of Indian Affairs, 1891*, 2 vols. (Washington, D.C.: Government Printing Office, 1891), 2:326–27. Data respecting

the uses and importance of Indian testimony appear in Jerome A. Greene, comp. and ed., *Lakota and Cheyenne: Indian Views of the Great Sioux War, 1876–1877* (Norman: University of Oklahoma Press, 1994), pp. xxi–xxiii. It has been suggested that Lakota veterans of Wounded Knee perhaps contrived compliant rather than defiant narratives of their recollections of the massacre. Jeffrey Ostler, *The Plains Sioux and U.S. Colonialism from Lewis and Clark to Wounded Knee* (Cambridge: Cambridge University Press, 2004), p. 340. This most likely would have occurred during the 1920s through 1940s as impending compensation legislation promoted the creation of survivors' organizations at the Pine Ridge and Cheyenne River Indian reservations.

4. Alice Ghost Horse, "A True Story of What Happened at Wounded Knee in December 1890," trans. Sidney Keith, *Twin Light Trail* 2 (1992): 11–14; "Paul High Back's Version of the Disaster of Dec. 29, 1890, at Wounded Knee, as Told to John Williamson," *Wi-iyohi: Monthly Bulletin of the South Dakota Historical Society* 10 (1 June 1956): 1–4. Army plans called for removing Big Foot and his people not to Pine Ridge Agency but to Gordon, Nebraska, where they would be placed on a waiting train bound for Omaha to remove them completely from the reservation environment so that their presence would not unduly influence other Lakotas. Greene, *American Carnage*, pp. 216–17, 224.

5. "Joseph Horn Cloud's Interview," in Richard E. Jensen, ed., *The Indian Interviews of Eli S. Ricker, 1903–1919* (Lincoln: University of Nebraska Press, 2005), p. 199; Ghost Horse, "A True Story of What Happened at Wounded Knee," 11–14; "Long Bull's Tale," *Washington Evening Star*, 28 Jan. 1891. This principal medicine man has been identified by several names, including Sits Straight but also Yellow Bird, Black Fox, and Good Thunder, among others. He had been haranguing the soldiers for some time preceding the outbreak of the shooting in the council area. *See* Greene, *American Carnage*, pp. 227–28.

6. "Joseph Horn Cloud's Interview," pp. 199–200.

7. Ibid., pp. 200–201. A statement prepared by Lakota survivors in September 1915 supported this unfolding scenario. It stated that the men were called to council at 8 a.m. and that the "army leader that met Big Foot yesterday [Major Samuel M. Whitside, Seventh Cavalry] said: Yesterday when I saw you, I seen that all of you men had guns. You will give me those guns." The men brought forth guns, some from the camp. "As they were putting their guns in the pile someone blew a whistle and all the army men loaded their guns as one." Then "an army leader sitting atop a dark bay horse gave the order to shoot and they started shooting" (Statement entitled "Dec. 29, 1890," signed by Peter One Skunk, Jessie Sunka Luzahan [Jessie Running Horse?], Alex High Hawk, Charles Blue Arm, Solomon Afraid of Enemy, and Daniel Blue Hair, Walter M. Camp Manuscripts, Lilly Library, Indiana University, Bloomington).

8. Iron Hail (Dewey Beard), interview with Dr. Melvin R. Gilmore, in "The Truth of the Wounded Knee Massacre," in *American Indian Magazine* 5 (Oct.–Dec. 1917): 249, and "A Massacre Survivor Speaks...," at http://www.dickshovel.com/DwyBrd.html; Horn Cloud, in Jensen, *Indian Interviews*, p. 201.

9. "Statement of Frog, of Big Foot's Band," 7 Jan. 1891 (interpreted by Philip F. Wells, witnessed by Reverend Charles Smith Cook), in National Archives (NA) Publication 983, "Sioux Campaign, 1890–91," Roll 1, pp. 717–18, copy in the Thomas Odell Collection, Leland D. Case Library, Special Collections, Black Hills State University, Spearfish, S.Dak.

10. "Statement of Help Them," 7 Jan. 1891 (interpreted by Philip F. Wells, witnessed by Reverend Charles Smith Cook), in NA Publication 983, "Sioux Campaign, 1890–91," Roll 1, pp. 717–18.

11. "Statement of Hehakawanyakapi," ca. 1891 (signed by the Reverend Charles Smith Cook and Philip F. Wells), Philip F. Wells Materials, D6, F41, Thomas Odell Collection. The accounts of Frog, Help Them, and Hehakawanyakapi also appeared in Philip F. Wells, "Ninety-Six Years among the Indians of the North West," *North Dakota History* 15 (Oct. 1948): 290–93.

12. Spotted Horse's remark is in "Account Given by Indians of the Fight at Wounded Knee, South Dakota, December 29, 1890," 11 Feb. 1891, in *Report of the Commissioner of Indian Affairs, 1891*, 2:180 (this document is also reproduced in James Mooney, "The Ghost-Dance Religion and the Sioux Outbreak of 1890," in *Fourteenth Annual Report of the Bureau of Ethnology to the Secretary of the Smithsonian Institution, 1892–93*, pp. 641–1136 [Washington, D.C.: Government Printing Office, 1896]); "Account of John Ghost Bear," 1 Nov. 1928, in National Archives (NA) at Kansas City, Record Group (RG) 75, Department of the Interior, Bureau of Indian Affairs, Pine Ridge Agency, Main Decimal Files, 1900–1965, NA Identifier 285586, File 053, Historical Data 1927–32, Box 172 (including quotation). Ghost Bear appears on "Copy of Muster Roll of Company C, Ogallala Indian Scouts, Recru[i]ted at Pine Ridge, So. Dak.," 27 Nov. 1890 to 30 Apr. 1891, p. 9, NA at Kansas City, RG 75, Bureau of Indian Affairs, Pine Ridge Agency, Main Decimal Files, 1900–1965, NA Identifier 285586, Decimal Code 650, Indians as Scouts, Box 657; Dog Chief account through Black Elk in John G. Neihardt, *The Sixth Grandfather: Black Elk's Teachings Given to John G. Neihardt*, ed. Raymond J. DeMallie (Lincoln: University of Nebraska Press, 1984), pp. 270–71.

13. "Paul High Back's Version of the Disaster of Dec. 29, 1890, at Wounded Knee," p. 2; Interview, Andrew Good Thunder, 12 July 1912, Box 6, Folder 14, pp. 521–32, Envelope 90, Camp Manuscripts.

14. Account of Zella Vespucia in *Washington Evening Star*, 27 Jan. 1891.

15. Joseph Horn Cloud's statement of 24 Oct. 1913, in Gilmore, "The Truth of the Wounded Knee Massacre," p. 247; "Paul High Back's Version of the Disaster of Dec.

29, 1890, at Wounded Knee," pp. 2–3; "Dewey Beard Interview," in Jensen, *Indian Interviews*, p. 224.

16. Iron Hail in Jensen, *Indian Interviews,* p. 222; Horn Cloud, ibid., p. 201.

17. "Account of John Ghost Bear," 1 Nov. 1928, in NA at Kansas City, RG 75, Bureau of Indian Affairs, Pine Ridge Agency, Main Decimal Files, 1900–1965, NA Identifier 285586, File 053, Historical Data 1927–32, Box 172.

18. Ghost Horse, "A True Story of What Happened at Wounded Knee," pp. 11–14.

19. Ibid.

20. Iron Hail quotations in Gilmore, "Truth of the Wounded Knee Massacre" (statement of 27 Nov. 1913), p. 250; and Jensen, *Indian Interviews,* pp. 223–24.

21. Iron Hail in Jensen, *Indian Interviews,* p. 225. For more on Iron Hail/Dewey Beard and his experiences, *see* Robert M. Utley, "Wounded Knee and Other Dark Images: The West of Dewey Horn Cloud," *American West: The Magazine of Western History* 16 (May/June 1979): 4–11.

22. Account of White Lance, in James H. McGregor, *The Wounded Knee Massacre from the Viewpoint of the Sioux* (Baltimore, Md.: Wirth Brothers, 1940), pp. 118–19.

23. Account of James Pipe on Head, ibid., pp. 108–9.

24. Account of Rough Feather, ibid., pp. 109–11.

25. Account of Mrs. Mousseau (Medicine Woman), ibid., pp. 113–14.

26. Account by Mrs. Mousseau given on 29 Oct. 1913, in Gilmore, "The Truth of the Wounded Knee Massacre," pp. 251–52. If there were indeed heroes on the army side at Wounded Knee, they most certainly were among the Indian scouts who tried to protect and save some of their people when things got out of hand. *See also* the statement of the Lakota scout White Buffalo, who maintained that "it was the insulting and overbearing conduct of a certain captain . . . that precipitated the trouble." He stated that the Indians had been "subject[ed] to insults of the greatest character" and that "white man shoot Indian first" (*Kansas City Star,* 10 Feb. 1891).

27. Account by Edward Owl King in McGregor, *The Wounded Knee Massacre,* pp. 116–17.

28. Account of Nellie Knife, ibid., pp. 138–39.

29. Account of Mrs. Rough Feather, ibid., pp. 127–28.

30. Account of Henry Jackson, ibid., pp. 119–20.

31. Account of John Little Finger, ibid., pp. 120–22.

32. Account of Peter Stand, ibid., pp. 123–24; accounts of Dog Chief and James High Hawk, ibid., pp. 133–36.

33. Account of Charley Blue Arm, ibid., p. 138.

34. Elaine Goodale Eastman, *Sister to the Sioux: The Memoirs of Elaine Goodale Eastman, 1885-91,* ed. Kay Graber (Lincoln: University of Nebraska Press, 1978), p. 160.

35. John G. Neihardt, comp., *Black Elk Speaks: Being the Life Story of a Holy Man of the Oglala Sioux*, annotated by Raymond J. DeMallie (Albany: State University of New York Press, 2008), pp. 207 (first quotation), 210 (second quotation); Neihardt, *The Sixth Grandfather*, p. 274 (third quotation).

36. Neihardt, *Black Elk Speaks*, pp. 207–14 (including first quotation); Neihardt, *The Sixth Grandfather*, pp. 273–74 (including second quotation). (For a critique of Black Elk's remembrances, *see* Michael F. Steltenkamp, *Nicholas Black Elk: Medicine Man, Missionary, Mystic* [Norman: University of Oklahoma Press, 2009], pp. 69–70.) Philip Wells maintained that, by and large, "women and children did not fight [at Wounded Knee]. They were busy getting away in order to save their lives." "Comments of Philip F. Wells," in Thomas E. Odell, "Comments on Mr. W. R. Leigh's information regarding the Wounded Knee battle," in Odell Papers, D6, F41, Case Library. Within months, Brule chief Hollow Horn Bear at Rosebud Agency suggested that some of the Wounded Knee Indian dead were, in fact, mixed-blood children fathered years earlier by soldiers at Fort Laramie. *Army and Navy Register*, 14 Mar. 1891.

37. Ghost Horse, "A True Story of What Happened at Wounded Knee in December 1890," pp. 13–14 (quotation); "As Narrated by Short Bull," translated by George Trager (1891), manuscript in the Buffalo Bill Museum and Grave Archives at Lookout Mountain, Denver, Colo.; "Paul High Back's Version of the Disaster of Dec. 29, 1890, at Wounded Knee," pp. 2–3. For accounts of other Lakotas who were present at Wounded Knee, see those of Louise Weasel Bear, George Running Hawk, Bertha Kills Close to Lodge, Donald Blue Hair, Afraid of the Enemy, Frank Sits Poor, Richard Afraid of Hawk, and Joseph Black Hair, in McGregor, *The Wounded Knee Massacre*, and that of Ellis Standing Bear in Standing Bear, *My People the Sioux*, ed. E. A. Brininstool (Boston: Houghton Mifflin Company, 1928), pp. 231–32. Hearsay or secondary accounts passed down from participants and eyewitnesses, while perhaps not possessing the immediacy and likely accuracy of persons who were on the scene in 1890, nonetheless possess ephemeral value that can be interpretively useful among families in recalling, conveying, and preserving recollections of what happened. Among the best are "Celane Not Help Him," in regard to Iron Hail/Dewey Beard in Sarah Penman, comp. and ed., *Honor the Grandmothers: Dakota and Lakota Women Tell Their Stories* (St. Paul: Minnesota Historical Society Press, 2000); Richard E. Jensen and R. Eli Paul, National Register of Historic Places Nomination Form for Wounded Knee National Historic Landmark, 6 Dec. 1990, with statements of Celane Not Help Him, re: Iron Hail/Dewey Beard, 1 Aug. 1990; Leonard Little Finger, re: John Little Finger, 14 July 1990; and Birgil Kills Straight, re: Daniel White Lance, 14 July 1990. *See also* Celane Not Help Him, re: Iron Hail/Dewey Beard, *Lakota Times*, 6 Oct. 1990; Eugene Wounded Horse as told to Will Spindler, "Dewy Girl Was There," *Real West* 11 (July 1968): 20–21, 54; Turning Hawk, Ameri-

can Horse, and George Sword (none of whom were present at Wounded Knee), in *Report of the Commissioner of Indian Affairs, 1891*, 2 vols. (Washington, D.C.: Government Printing Office, 1891), 1:179–81; "Report of Elaine Goodale," 12 Jan. 1891, in *Washington Post*, 17 Jan. 1891. Although of a secondary nature, the latter two citations contain solid information about Wounded Knee taken close to the event from persons who were present. A useful though somewhat editorialized montage incorporating both participant and hearsay Lakota accounts appears in William S. E. Coleman, *Voices of Wounded Knee* (Lincoln: University of Nebraska Press, 2000), pp. 279–341.

38. "Data on monument and notes of Battlefield and fight from Indian side (1910)," Box 5, Folder 13, Envelope 78, Camp Manuscripts. It is clear today that the Hotchkiss fire did not take place until the cavalry shooting in the council area was finished.

39. Jerome A. Greene, ed., *Soldiering in the Shadow of Wounded Knee: The 1891 Diary of Private Hartford G. Clark, Sixth U.S. Cavalry* (Norman, Okla.: Arthur H. Clark Company, 2016), p. 34 (first quotation); author's interview with Leonard Little Finger, 21 Apr. 2010, Sacred Hoop School, Oglala, S.Dak. (second quotation). For discussion of the numbers of Indians present and killed, *see* Mooney, "Ghost Dance Religion," pp. 870–71. For the army's February 1891 estimate of Indian casualties, *see* Greene, *American Carnage*, pp. 399–401. An unavoidably imprecise tabulation containing more than 800 entries that nonetheless helps personalize the Lakotas' presence at Wounded Knee appears in Richard E. Jensen, "Big Foot's Followers at Wounded Knee," *Nebraska History* 71 (Fall 1990): 201–9, and accounts for perhaps 71 wounded Lakotas who survived. Among early listings of casualty data, *see* especially Perain P. Palmer, "Number and names of Indians absent and not drawing Rations at Cheyenne River Agency, S.D., December 22, 1890" (which includes names of heads of families and sizes of families), 28 Dec. 1890, NA at Kansas City, RG 75, Cheyenne River, Book 364; "Approximate Census of the Sioux Indians belonging to the Cheyenne River reservation who were in the battle of Wounded Knee and as yet at Pine Ridge Agency S.D., taken January 30, 1891" (lists name, sex, age, whether living or dead, and includes a Black Fox, age thirty-three, as "Dead"), NA, RG 75, copy in H76.24, Folder 16, Box 3564A, Wounded Knee Compensation Papers, South Dakota State Historical Society, Pierre; Joseph Horn Cloud, "Names of those killed at the Wounded Knee Massacre, Pine Ridge Agency, South Dakota, December 29, 1890" (ca. 1907), in Jensen, *Indian Interviews*, pp. 204–8 (also included in Donald F. Danker, ed., *The Wounded Knee Interviews of Eli S. Ricker* [reprint from *Nebraska History* 62 (Summer 1981): 164–79], pp. 176–79); "List of Indians Killed and Wounded at Sioux Massacre, December 29, 1890," with collateral papers, filed by Joseph Horn Cloud, 14 Apr. 1920 (incorporates lists compiled in 1917 and 1918 and includes people living at Pine Ridge, Cheyenne River, and

Standing Rock), copy in Box 3564A, Wounded Knee Compensation Papers. *See also* James W. Wengert, comp., "Wounded Knee Killed or Subsequently Died of Wounds," in James Wengert Military Medical Collection, Pritzker Military Library, Chicago, Ill.

For insights into the afterlife of the Lakota experience at Wounded Knee, emphasizing the event's meaning and enduring significance within tribal history and culture as well as the people's struggle to indemnify their losses during the decades following the massacre, *see* especially David W. Grua, *Surviving Wounded Knee: The Lakotas and the Politics of Memory* (New York: Oxford University Press, 2016).

7 : Remembering the Buffalo Soldiers

Memorials to Black Soldiers of the Indian-War Era

FRANK N. SCHUBERT

Historical monuments and their meaning have become widely discussed and divisive subjects in recent years. These conversations focus largely on the legitimacy of celebrating prominent figures of the southern Confederacy but also include questions about memorials ranging from Christopher Columbus to Pocahontas as well as the troubling issue of how to mark sites of lynchings. This essay concerns a related but so far less controversial subject: monuments to "buffalo soldiers," black soldiers who served in the Regular Army between the Civil War of 1861–65 and American entry into World War I in 1917.[1]

In considering this subject, it is important to start with a few observations about the buffalo soldiers themselves, who they were, what they did, and why I think they were important. Just over 11 percent of the small Indian-fighting army was black, and this was important. In 1866, the Regular Army, in at least tacit recognition of the black soldier's significant service during the Civil War, for the first time made a place for him—in the Ninth and Tenth Cavalry regiments and the Twenty-Fourth and Twenty-Fifth Infantry regiments. It was a segregated place in which it was almost impossible to become an officer, but it was a place. Blacks had earlier served as volunteer soldiers but never as members of the Regular Army. From 1866 on, there would always be black soldiers in the United States Army.

They came to be called "buffalo soldiers," apparently because some Plains Indians saw a physical resemblance between their brown skin and curly hair and the buffalo. They fought in some of the major wars against Indians, most notably in the brutal campaign against the Apache leaders Victorio and Nana in 1879–81. They also did what all soldiers did in the West: they protected wagon trains, the mail, and telegraph lines, mapped new and unfamiliar territory, and built roads. Twenty-three buffalo soldiers received the Medal of Honor, then the only army decoration for bravery and now its highest, during the frontier wars or the campaign in Cuba in 1898. But mainly the buffalo soldiers represented the involvement of African Americans in the central drama of nineteenth-century American history: the nation's westward expansion and the dispossession of the American Indians that accompanied it. Buffalo soldiers were important because they served—and fought—right after the end of the era of slavery and staked a claim on citizenship through national service. As free men, they were mainstream participants in this national epic. Their statues and other commemorations are important reminders of their service. These memorials are also significant for what they show us about America today.

Students of history are accustomed to anomaly. We deal with human behavior, so paradox, contradiction, ambiguity, and perversity are familiar to us. Like other parts of human history, the American story has its share of irrationality and illogic, much of which is driven by the racism that remains a problem in our society.

Consider this. The Civil War, the great sectional conflict that tore the nation apart, was won by the Union with an army of about 2 million men. Roughly 10 percent of that army (between 180,000 and 200,000 individuals) was black. The victory is marked by thousands of public memorials—statues and sculptures in town squares, parks, and cemeteries.[2] Yet, during the great era of commemoration in the fifty years after the Civil War, just three of the many hundreds of memorials that were erected showed any black military figures. Two of those were obscure single figures surrounded by many white soldiers.[3] Only the Augustus Saint-Gaudens relief in Boston Common that celebrates the heroism of Robert Gould Shaw, the colonel of the black Fifty-Fourth Massachusetts Infantry, has black soldiers in a highly visible, even prominent position. The Saint-Gaudens masterpiece, with its realistic black infantrymen of varying height and appearance, was unveiled in 1897.[4]

The statuary of the vanquished Confederacy mirrored that of the victors. Both sides adopted the same model: a standing, uniformed and armed white common soldier. The symbolism is clear. We are looking at free (standing), legitimate (uniformed), powerful (armed) men. We are also looking at "our boys," volunteer soldiers from towns all across the nation, who joined locally recruited regiments such as the First Minnesota or the Nineteenth Virginia and whose sacrifice is celebrated in their home towns and counties.

The statue at the National Cemetery near the Antietam battlefield in Maryland, nicknamed *Old Simon*, was completed in 1874, shown at the Philadelphia centennial exhibition in 1876–78, and sent to Antietam in 1880. Its dimensions are mind-boggling. It is made of 27 pieces of granite weighing 250 tons. The figure alone is 21.5 feet tall and weighs 29 tons, and the structure, including the base, is 44 feet 7 inches tall. It is inscribed: "Not for themselves but for their country, September 17, 1862."[5] Aside from its monumental dimensions, it reflects all the conventions of the less-imposing statuary in local cemeteries and town squares by depicting a standing, uniformed, and armed white common soldier.

Erecting local monuments to white soldiers was a big business. The Muldoon Monument Company of Louisville, Kentucky, boasted that it made 905 Confederate monuments, and the American Bronze Foundry Company of staunchly Unionist Chicago advertised "Confederate Statues in Bronze." Generally speaking, statues were individually made, based on a standard model that could be altered in small ways to suit a client. All of the firms that produced them made both Union and Confederate statues.[6]

Unlike the Civil War, with its huge armies, the Indian wars of the next generation were fought by an army of about 25,000, about 1 to 2 percent of the size of the Civil War force. The soldiers were regulars, enlisted for specific terms of service, assigned to "U.S." regiments, and recruited nationwide. Westerners never developed ties to this small Regular Army that battled the Indians and protected them, so local incentive to celebrate their efforts and lives was lacking. The "victory" of the small Regular Army over the Indians, about which some Americans now feel pangs of guilt, generated almost no statuary showing black or white soldiers in the century following the final Indian disaster, the massacre at Wounded Knee, South Dakota, at the end of December 1890.[7]

Virtually all the markers and structures at more than 110 forts and battlefields involved freestanding historical markers or plaques on pyramids of stones or rectangular columns of rock.[8] One statue in the Civil War tradition at Fort McPherson, Nebraska, depicting a standing, uniformed and armed white common soldier, basically a smaller version of *Old Simon*, celebrated the role of the Seventh Iowa Volunteer Cavalry in bringing white settlement to Lincoln County, Nebraska. A statue of a mounted trooper at Fort Riley, Kansas, is based on Frederic Remington's drawing *Old Bill*. Because commemorative statuary is an urban phenomenon, this is no surprise; most of the battlefields are far from cities or even major highways.[9] Besides, the western fights, with few exceptions, were not of the epic scale of the Civil War. Moreover, the soldiers lacked the deep preexisting ties to the localities where they served. Western residents saw them as part of an entitlement, a deserved national subsidy for their pioneer endeavors. Although some soldiers stayed and became part of western society, they were not part of the community whose stores, bars, and whorehouses they patronized while on active service. They were part of a national subvention and not expected to interfere.[10] For all of these reasons, the monuments marking forts and battle sites and roadside markers generally lack human form and personification.[11] Commemorative displays rarely depict individuals. When they do, they show two-dimensional silhouettes or line drawings of modest size. A tradition of statuary like that of the Civil War never took hold.

But in 1977 came a new statue of a soldier. He was black, and his name was *Emmett*. The figure, designed by Rose Murray, showed a gritty trooper, maybe just in from a grueling desert patrol or a hard pursuit of bandits. Like the statues commemorating the Vietnam War that started to appear at the same time, he looked more realistic than heroic. Also like Vietnam statuary, he reflected a trend away from an all-white image of the armed forces toward "a more pluralistic vision of nationhood and the willingness to accord greater equality of recognition to African Americans and women."[12] This sturdy figure was eight feet tall and massive, weighing 24,000 pounds. For thirty years he guarded the front gate of Fort Huachuca, near the border in southern Arizona. In February 2007 he was moved to a centrally located traffic circle, which was renamed Buffalo Soldier Legacy Plaza during a local "Year of the Buffalo Soldier" celebra-

The first buffalo soldier statue erected in the West was Rose Murray's *Emmett* in 1977, who guarded the front gate of Fort Huachuca, Arizona. *Jeffry M. Platt Collection*

tion. Although he has moved, he is still the first buffalo soldier statue erected in the West.[13]

Eight more statues have appeared since 1992, all of black soldiers and all at western forts. What does this mean? Clearly statues do more than add visual interest to the landscape, make work for designers and sculptors, and lure tourists. They are also more than resting places for pigeons. Statuary helps illuminate a society and its culture by sending messages about three things: (1) the position of blacks in American society; (2) the changing image of the Indian and the Indian wars; and (3) how American society sees itself.

The rise of the buffalo soldier to prominence began in the 1960s, the period of the Civil War centennial and the Civil Rights revolution. Some African Americans retained knowledge of the military heritage, but only later did the nation at large become familiar with the buffalo soldiers. The process started in the late 1950s, with Dudley Taylor Cornish's book *The Sable Arm*, about black Civil War soldiers, and continued with John Ford's *Sergeant Rutledge* (1960), a film of subtlety and insight about a black sergeant accused of rape and murder.[14] The civil rights movement also provoked reconsideration of the Civil War and encouraged a new focus on black soldiers. The 1960s brought expanded interest in black history in general, the establishment of black studies programs in universities, and an interest in buffalo soldiers.[15] William Leckie's book *The Buffalo Soldiers: A Narrative of the Negro Cavalry in the West* appeared in 1967. "The Buffalo Soldiers," a song recorded by two rhythm-and-blues groups, the Flamingos and the Persuasions, recalled the soldiers' heroics on the frontier and in the war against Spain in 1898 and plaintively asked the buffalo soldiers, "Will you survive in this new land?"[16]

In the 1990s, after two decades of gradually increasing interest and the appearance of a growing body of literature, monuments to buffalo soldiers were erected in several places, most notably at Fort Leavenworth, Kansas, where several companies of the Tenth Cavalry had been organized in 1866 and 1867. On 25 July 1992, General Colin Powell dedicated a larger-than-life statue of a mounted trooper there by sculptor Eddie Dixon. Powell, a black four-star army general and the first African American officer to serve as chairman of the Joint Chiefs of Staff, was the military advisor to the president of the United States. Deeply interested in the history of black participation in the armed forces, Powell considered himself "the descendant of those Buffalo Soldiers . . . and all the black men and women who have served the nation in uniform."[17]

Powell's appearance at Fort Leavenworth was pivotal to an expanding awareness of buffalo soldiers. When he spoke at the 1992 dedication to an audience in which black veterans of the segregated army and uniformed buffalo-soldier reenactors were conspicuous, major television networks carried the ceremony. Powell reminded the nation of the tradition of black military service: "From the beginning of our nation, African Americans answered the call to arms in defense of America whenever that call came." After the establishment of the regiments of black regulars after the Civil War, "African Americans would henceforth always be in uniform, challenging the conscience of the nation, posing the question, 'How could they be allowed to defend the cause of freedom, to defend the nation, if they, themselves, were to be denied the benefits of being American?'" Powell acknowledged that he, the highest-ranking officer in the armed forces and in the eyes of many a hero of the 1991 war against Iraq, owed a debt to the black soldiers who had gone before him and challenged young people not to forget the soldiers' sacrifice and their service.[18]

Powell put his finger on something important. The acceptance of black soldiers into the Regular Army did in fact represent a building block in an ongoing struggle to achieve equality. The effort took a long time to bear fruit and even contained a step backward in that it was also a precedent for segregation, both in the government and in the society at large. But it was in effect an experimental—albeit unintended—step with broad positive implications, for it ultimately helped make legal equality impossible to avoid. Conservative objectors to the use of the military to encourage social change, including those who recently opposed the inclusion of women and then resisted inclusion of open homosexuals and transsexuals, should bear this in mind. The military has historically been a successful instrument of social change, starting with emancipation itself. After all, it was only through the force of Union arms that slavery was abolished in the United States. And in the twentieth century the armed forces desegregated several years before segregated schools even began grudgingly to admit blacks, again sometimes only after military intervention. Even when military leaders resist and deny its legitimacy, they ultimately salute, obey, and enforce national social policy. They did with black service members, they are doing so with women, and they will do so with homosexuals and transsexuals.

The well-publicized ceremony at Fort Leavenworth was accompanied by declarations by both houses of Congress that 28 July 1992 was "Buffalo Soldier Day."[19] In the wake of the observance also came what James Leiker called "a veritable explosion of Buffalo Soldiers commemorations including museum displays, documentaries, newspaper and journal articles, and reenactment societies."[20] The statue also became a significant part of Fort Leavenworth's own identity, adorning local telephone directories, postcards, and souvenir refrigerator magnets. The anonymity of the buffalo soldiers in the United States ended nationally in the summer of 1992.

In the 1990s, the period of the dedication of these statues, buffalo soldiers also entered popular culture. Their images appeared on T-shirts galore, coffee mugs, and a postage stamp, and they became the subjects of romance novels, children's books, plays, feature films, and popular songs. Memorial Day ceremonies celebrated their bravery, while reenactors dressed and paraded in frontier attire, imitating these soldiers. They were featured in more than three hundred books and articles, commemorative events, and the naming of landmarks and streets in their honor, not to mention action figures, a jigsaw puzzle, greeting cards, and even a necktie offered by J. C. Penney and made in China. The list is almost interminable. When I made a presentation on buffalo soldiers at the Smithsonian's National Museum of American History in 2001, I took along—and left as a donation—a box of this stuff accumulated over my years of research, including a two-foot-tall, black-painted plaster copy of the *Emmett* statue. By the end of the decade the buffalo soldier was a well-known and widely familiar cultural icon.

Monuments appeared at other western posts where black soldiers had served. Two were installed in New Mexico at historic posts that were no longer active. The life-sized bronze figure at Fort Bayard, New Mexico, representing Medal of Honor recipient Corporal Clinton Greaves and designed by Gregory Whipple of nearby Silver City, New Mexico, was also dedicated in the summer of 1992. Understandably, it never got the attention that Powell's presence brought to Leav-

The life-size, bronze figure at Fort Bayard, New Mexico, represented Medal of Honor recipient Corporal Clinton Greaves; designed by Gregory Whipple of nearby Silver City, New Mexico, and dedicated in 1992.
Mark Erickson Collection

Dedicated in 1999 at Fort Bliss, Texas, sculptor Jimmie Bemont's sculpture showed a corporal of the Ninth Cavalry engaged in a running fight. *Fort Bliss Museum, United States Army*

enworth.[21] Reynaldo ("Sonny") Rivera's *The Sentinel* was unveiled in July 1994 at Fort Selden near Las Cruces in southern New Mexico.[22]

Sonny Rivera designed a more controversial statue that was unveiled the same year: the twelve-foot-tall Albuquerque likeness of Juan de Oñate, known as the last conquistador. The monument provoked Hispanic pride and Indian fury, focused on the story of how Oñate had ordered his men to chop off the right feet of two dozen Acoma captives. The Indians may have waited four centuries, but they got their revenge. In 1998, on the 400th anniversary of Oñate's arrival, they took a power saw to the statue's right foot and sliced it off, boot, stirrup, spur and all. Oñate Monument and Visitor Center director Estevan Arellano had a new foot—maybe one could call it a prosthesis—attached. "Give me a break," he groaned. "It was 400 years ago. It's OK to hold a grudge, but for 400 years?"[23]

The next monument to buffalo soldiers was dedicated in 1999 at Fort Bliss, the headquarters of Army Air Defense Artillery outside El Paso, Texas. Sculptor Jimmie Bemont's design, based on artist Bob Snead's painting, showed Corporal John Ross of the Ninth Cavalry engaged in a running fight with three Mescalero Apache warriors. The irony of the statue's location near the Robert E. Lee gate might not have been lost on at least some of the visitors to the site.[24]

Another monument to black soldiers' service in the West, a very long time in the making because of the difficulty in raising money, stands outside the main gate at Francis E. Warren Air Force Base, near Cheyenne, Wyoming, the Fort D. A. Russell of the Indian-wars era. Planning for this monument started in the early 1990s. Eddie Dixon, whose sculpture graced the grounds of Fort Leavenworth, designed a statue of a mounted trooper that was used for marketing in 1995, but that effort foundered. The finished product, based on a pedestrian design by Chris Navarro, was not erected and dedicated until June 2007.[25] Navarro, a former rodeo cowboy from Casper, Wyoming, who worked out of a studio in Sedona, Arizona, called himself "the Remington of Our Time in the world of Western Bronze Art."[26] The basis for that claim is not clear to me.

By 2011, the statues dedicated to buffalo soldiers numbered nine. New ones were installed in Junction City, outside Fort Riley, Kansas in 2000, at Lawton next to Fort Sill, Oklahoma, in 2010, and in Albuquerque, New Mexico, in 2011. From Emmett to Corporal Ross, the memorials carried elements of archetypal Civil War statues, showing standing (or mounted), uniformed, and armed common soldiers—masculine, legitimate, powerful figures.[27] Yet, they were different; the Civil War statues, artifacts of the late nineteenth and early twentieth centuries, showed men in reflective poses, standing at rest, perhaps lost in thought about the carnage they had seen or the comrades they had lost or maybe the consequences of their service.

With the exception of Rose Murray's *Emmett*, the buffalo soldier statues of the late twentieth century all show men in action, on duty, ready, alert, and even fighting. They do not conform to a single pattern but are far more individualized than the cookie-cutter images

The monument at Fort D. A. Russell, now Francis E. Warren Air Force Base, Wyoming, was erected and dedicated in 2007. *Public Affairs Office, Francis E. Warren Air Force Base*

that commemorate the Civil War. The differences can be explained perhaps by our distance from the wars they show or perhaps by the nature of those wars and our own reaction to them. Only recently have most Americans come to consider the Indian conflicts as in some way deplorable, while the Civil War has always been seen as a great national tragedy with devastating losses that all could feel. Both groups of monuments are representational and therefore realistic, but the buffalo-soldier statuary, with its heroically posed soldiers, celebrates warfare rather than reflects on it. At a time when it is commonplace to label all military service members as heroes, perhaps this should be no surprise. In any case, beyond the details of the sculptures, whatever the postures and body languages of the figures themselves, lies an overwhelming fact. Just as the large number of Civil War monuments gave American nationalism of the time the face of the common white soldier, so the wave of buffalo-soldier statuary at the end of the twentieth century added the face of the common black soldier to the picture of the expansion of post–Civil War America.

These statues documented the political strength of black America. The new wave of memorial sculptures, highlighting black military contributions, bespoke a new time. The new monuments expressed the significant position of African Americans in the body politic and particularly in the military services at the end of the twentieth century. As Kirk Savage, historian of Civil War memorialization, noted, "Public monuments do not arise as if by natural law to celebrate the deserving; they are built by people with sufficient power to marshal (or impose) public consent for their erection."[28] Influence and wealth are prerequisites for raising money, buying land, retaining a sculptor, and getting public attention and approval for such an enterprise. The wave of public monuments marked much more than the arrival of the buffalo soldier in American culture; it signaled the arrival of African Americans at a new level of political strength and influence.

It should be noted that other manifestations of this political clout also concerned historical interpretation. The Consolidated Appropriations Act of 1999, which provided funding for the national park system, required the secretary of the interior to encourage park managers of Civil War battle sites to "recognize and include in all of their public displays and multi-media educational presentations the unique role the institution of slavery played in causing the Civil War and its role, if any, at the individual battle sites." The measure was introduced by Congressman Jesse Jackson Jr., Democrat of Chicago.[29]

But these statues are not just about the political clout of black Americans. They were, are, and will be about the history of the United States. After all, we are not just talking about black history; we are talking about American history. André Malraux wrote that "a culture will be judged by its statues." Gary Wills agreed, noting that "what we choose to remember in stone [or bronze] tells us who we are, or want to be" and that "if any culture is to be understood, historians must read it by judging what it chose to honor." Michael Kammen's observation that we tend to "historicize the present in a somewhat facile, sometimes inadvertent way" may also be pertinent, because I do not think the purpose of this statuary was to present an image of the Indian wars as conflict between red and black peoples. So, while we are adapting our recall to meet current needs, as David Lowenthal wrote, and making "the past intelligible in the light of present circumstances," we could be leaving posterity a hugely distorted and ironic image of the frontier wars.[30]

The Indian wars had a face before this wave of buffalo-soldier statuary and commemoration, even if it was rarely chiseled in the stone of public sculpture.[31] It was a white face, framed by blond, usually longish hair, and belonged to George Armstrong Custer, killed by the Cheyennes and Sioux with 225 of his men at the Little Big Horn River in Montana on 25 June 1876. Custer's defeat happened just days before 4 July 1876, the one hundredth anniversary of the declaration of American independence, celebrated in Philadelphia with a huge exposition showing the growing wealth, sophistication, and maturity of the nation. Imagine the shock of the news that more than two hundred soldiers of this rich, sprawling nation had been killed by people considered mere savages. The reports were devastating, and the country needed an uplifting myth. Poets, novelists, and painters promptly turned George Custer into a gallant martyr in the spread of civilization.[32]

Perhaps Custer will remain the personification of the Indian-fighting army. He has been at the center of the American view of the frontier army for so long that he will be very difficult to dislodge. Custer's widow, Elizabeth Bacon Custer, promoted his reputation with maniacal energy. He was, she wrote, her "bright particular star," and she made sure that his fiery point of light continued to shine long after his death. His impact—and hers—is reflected in a staggering volume of Custeriana, including nearly two thousand paintings and illustrations and an amazing forty-six films.[33] Some consider Custer a martyr who, depending on one's viewpoint, died for the advancement of Western civilization or for the sins of that civilization in its treatment of the Indians. Either way, he died for a cause, not just as a result of his stupidity, lack of knowledge of the enemy, or impetuosity.[34] In Western Christian culture, martyrdom is a very powerful idea.

Today Custer's position is waning, at least a little. The Indians have been chipping away at his preeminence at the Little Bighorn Battlefield since 1976, the year of the centennial commemoration of his death, with a confrontational presence at the site itself. They achieved a major symbolic victory when the battlefield park, known for many years as Custer National Monument, was renamed the Little Bighorn National Monument in 1991. The argument against Custer emphasized his centrality as the symbol of the white view in which the conquest of the West represented the triumph of civilization over savagery.[35] However, these passionate opponents of the Custer myth sustained his central role. The Indians never attacked him as an incompetent commander who led his troops to their death out of ignorance, vanity, and stupidity. Such a position would diminish the achievements of their ancestors. As far as the Indians were concerned, when they beat Custer, they rubbed out the army's best.[36] Custer has therefore gone from the great hero—the Boy General, Bravest of the Brave, Last of the Cavaliers, and so on—to "supreme white anti-hero."[37] And Indians, who for many years had little impact on public opinion, are now showing that they too have political clout.

Still, Custer's position as the archetype of the Indian-fighting army is weakening, partly because of Indian attacks on his legacy and the conquest he represented, but also because the buffalo soldier is rising as a competing model. The proliferation of statues, along with other images of the black regular, suggests the possibility that one day the face of American nationalism during the Indian-war period may turn out to be not the face of Custer but the face of the black common soldier. After all, heroes do not have to endure forever. They can fade away, and there is no reason why Custer's fame should continue undiminished. As Lowenthal wrote more than forty years ago, "Memory not only conserves the past but adjusts recall to current needs. Instead of remembering exactly what was, we make the past intelligible in the light of present circumstances."[38] Sometimes we improve the past to suit our current interests or needs, and one of the needs today is for nonwhite heroes.[39] Just as surely as the permanence of Custer's stature is not guaranteed, there is no reason why Custer should not be replaced by a collective entity such as the archetypical frontier soldier, the buffalo soldier.[40]

But wait! As the face of this expansionist nationalism becomes the face of buffalo soldiers fighting Indians, two ironies emerge. First, nearly 90 percent of the frontier army was, in fact, white. Second, the new image is of one nonwhite group fighting and defeating another nonwhite group in the service of white goals. This is not what the promoters of the buffalo soldier heritage had in mind when they set out to build these new statues in the West and directly clashes with the part of the buffalo-soldier myth that posits Indian respect for the troopers. Viewing the world from a Rainbow Coalition perspective, which assumes that all people of color share values, interests, and grievances stemming from having been discriminated against if not oppressed by whites, they are clearly troubled by the problem. Those who promote the preeminence of the buffalo soldier have dealt with the issue of black-soldier relations with Indians by asserting a dual myth: that black soldiers contributed disproportionately to the winning of the West, even as they developed an empathy and mutual respect with the Indians on the basis of their shared nonwhiteness. This is indeed a tough and contradictory proposition.

The mythic view that the soldiers and the Indians shared some sort of bond has two foundations. One is the notion that the Indians called the soldiers "buffalo soldiers" as a sign of respect for their fighting abilities. The buffalo was special, even sacred, to the Plains tribes, this line of reasoning says; therefore, the Indians would not have called the troopers buffalo soldiers if they had not meant it respectfully, so the phrase must mean more than a reference to brown skin or nappy hair. The other foundation is modern Rainbow Coalition wishful thinking that projects backward into the nineteenth century the feeling that nonwhites share a common bond based on their relationship to a common oppressor. The myth arises from the problem of rationalizing black participation in white conquest while deflecting the guilt inherent in that role. The alleged mutual respect and empathy that soldiers and Indians supposedly felt resists proof because, although it is so reassuring, documentation in support or opposition to it is lacking.

Unfortunately for the mythmakers, their effort ignores the reality of the buffalo-soldier reaction to the Indians, which reflected an unbridgeable cultural gap. This is worth elaboration: buffalo soldiers came from a monotheistic, English-speaking, agrarian-industrial culture; the Indians were seminomadic warrior-hunters who spoke many languages, none of which was English. Their religious practices —shamanism, supernatural visions, self-mutilation, and human sacrifice—were unfamiliar, even repellent to the soldiers. The black soldiers' reactions to the Indians mirrored the prevailing white racism. Black soldiers used the same dismissive epithets: "hostile tribes," "naked savages," and "redskins." They also indulged in the same racist caricatures that whites employed. Reminiscent of whites' use of "blackface" to denigrate and stereotype African Americans, a black private named Robinson, for example, went to a masquerade ball at Fort Bayard in 1894 mockingly dressed as "an idiotic Indian squaw."[41]

The response of black soldiers to Indians should be interpreted with care. Black soldiers in the generation after slavery longed for inclusion in the society at large. That society was certainly racist, and soldiers' use of bigoted terms and stereotypes may show no more than their acquiescence in the larger cultural order, a phenomenon that Joel Kovel calls "metaracism."[42] So, when a black soldier in 1890 called a Plains Indian "a voodoo nigger,"[43] he not only repeated the voice of a white soldier who called the Plains Indians in 1873 "red niggers;"[44] he also reflected the overall values of the culture in which he struggled to make his own place. By such usages, he hoped to ally himself with the dominant group.[45]

Both aspects of the mythical view, that the soldiers were the army's best and that they uniquely appreciated the Indians' plight, were articulated in the film *Buffalo Soldiers* (1997), directed by the well-known actor Danny Glover. This film, aired by Turner Network Television, was meant to be taken seriously, as evidenced by the "Educator's Guide" that was released with it.[46] It portrayed the buffalo soldiers as so able that they did something no United States soldiers, black or white, ever managed to do: surprise and capture Victorio and his band of Warm Springs Apaches. With the Apaches under their control, the troopers did something else that no United States soldiers, black or white, ever did. After sympathetic conversations over coffee, in which soldiers and warriors expressed their mutual understanding of the oppression that each experienced at the hands of whites, the troopers let the Apaches go. This fantasy insulted both parties. The Apaches, who were expert trackers and scouts, never allowed themselves to be encircled by American soldiers of any color. The buffalo soldiers, had they been adept enough and lucky enough to have bagged Victorio, would never have let him go. The story might have consoled some people but did not reflect reality.[47] For all its faults, by the way, the Glover film is not the all-time-worst buffalo-soldier film. That distinction goes to *Soul Soldier* (1970), a film squarely in the Blaxploitation style.

American Indian advocates in the 1990s objected strongly to the attention given to the buffalo soldiers, particularly to the idea that their forebears and the soldiers shared a bond of respect or understanding. The issue of a postage stamp commemorating buffalo soldiers in 1994 catalyzed this dissent. United States Postal Service publicity materials asserted that the name "Buffalo Soldiers" had been "bestowed by Native Americans for the courage displayed on the battlefield" and that "the combat prowess, bravery, and courage on the battlefield of these black troopers inspired the Indians to call them Buffalo Soldiers."[48]

The first salvo of dissent came from Vernon Bellecourt of the American Indian Movement, a veteran of the 1973 Wounded Knee takeover on the Pine Ridge Indian Reservation. Writing in the newspaper *Indian Country Today*, a reliable forum for objections to glorification of buffalo soldiers, Bellecourt denied that the name reflected any "endearment or respect." As far as he was concerned, Plains Indians only applied the term "buffalo soldier" to "these marauding murderous cavalry units" because of "their dark skin and texture of their hair."[49] Such angry outbursts continued through the 1990s,[50] as did demonstrations at museum exhibits on buffalo-soldier history and other public observances. Just as the Leavenworth statue catalyzed public awareness of the buffalo soldier, so the stamp provoked substantial Indian resentment of the favorable publicity given to the troopers.[51]

What do we conclude about the statues and buffalo-soldier commemorations? Beyond the clear evidence of growing black political clout, underscored in 2008 by the election of Barack Obama as the first African American president, are issues of interaction among multiple racial and ethnic groups. As Leiker has shown in the case of buffalo soldiers stationed along the Rio Grande, race is not acted out in the United States on a binary basis between blacks and whites alone. Many others are involved, including Indians, Latinos, Asian Americans, and, as we have recently become sharply aware, Arab Americans. Interaction takes place among and between these groups, as well as between them and whites. In the case of the buffalo soldiers, the increasing media exposure and growing political power of the Indian rights movement that successfully promoted a negative view of Custer have made it a burden for anyone, black or white, to symbolize the Indian fighter and represent what many now consider to have been an exterminationist policy.[52] If the man who symbolizes the Indian fighter in history must have been evil, having carried out an immoral policy, then the buffalo soldier, whether he overtakes Custer as the symbol or not, also becomes the image of evil. To fend off this possibility, the myth of the buffalo soldier tries to co-opt the Indian challenge by asserting mutual respect.

As people confront these issues, the statues remain, silent but permanent reminders of the black presence in the Indian-fighting army. After all, these monuments, unlike the "Buffalo Soldiers" group sculpted in sand by Canadian Karen Fralich for the Jesolo (Italy) International Sand Sculpture Exhibition in 2007, are going to be there for a long time.[53] It is intriguing to speculate about their future as symbols of the frontier force. With no context of white-soldier statuary in the West to create perspective, is it possible that the face of the black soldier will become the dominant image of the Indian wars? Will these conflicts someday be seen as struggles between blacks and American Indians? Or will older white images, such as Custer paintings and films, offset that possibility, just as the recent appearance of buffalo-soldier statues has counterbalanced the traditional image of an all-white frontier army? As historians, maybe we should resist the desire to speculate about these possibilities and stick to what we know. One thing we do know is that the answer to the question "Buffalo Soldier, will you survive in this new land?" in the song is clear now. The buffalo soldier is thoroughly imbedded in American culture and has become a part of American history, and the reply is a resounding yes. As to the rest, we—or our grandchildren—shall see.

NOTES

1. An earlier version of this chapter was given as a public lecture at the National World War I Museum at Liberty Memorial, Kansas City, Missouri, on 8 Mar. 2008.

2. Kirk Savage, *Standing Soldiers, Kneeling Slaves: Race, War, and Monument in Nineteenth-Century America* (Princeton, N.J.: Princeton University Press, 1997), p. 3.

3. Black troops were almost completely ignored in public statuary, not just because they were black. With few exceptions, blacks fought in units called "United States Colored Troops," such as, for example, the Fourth United States Colored Infantry and First United States Colored Cavalry. They owed their allegiance more to the nation than to a particular locality, making local memorialization committees less likely to consider celebrating their service. Savage, *Standing Soldiers, Kneeling Slaves*, pp. 184–85, 187, 207.

4. On the design of the Shaw memorial, *see The Shaw Memorial: A Celebration of an American Masterpiece* (Conshohocken, Pa.: Eastern National, 1997). *See also* Savage, *Standing Soldiers, Kneeling Slaves*, pp. 198–204; and Martin H. Blatt, Thomas J. Brown, and Donald Yacavone, eds., *Hope & Glory: Essays on the Legacy of the 54th Massachusetts Regiment* (Amherst: University of Massachusetts Press, 2001).

5. Ted Alexander, "Old Simon," *Blue & Gray Magazine* 13 (Oct. 1995): 59–60.

6. Susan Cooke Soderberg, *"Lest We Forget": A Guide to Civil War Monuments in Maryland* (Shippensburg, Pa.: White Mane Publishing Co., 1995), pp. xxiv–xxv.

7. Kenneth E. Foote, *Shadowed Ground: America's Landscapes of Violence and Tragedy* (Austin: University of Texas Press, 1997), p. 322.

8. Herbert M. Hart, *Old Forts of the Northwest* (Seattle: Superior Publishing Co., 1963), p. 75.

9. James M. Mayo, *War Memorials as Political Landscape: American Experience and Beyond* (New York: Praeger, 1988), p. 148.

10. On the army's role in western development, *see* Michael L. Tate, *The Frontier Army in the Settlement of the West* (Norman: University of Oklahoma Press, 1999).

11. There is no comprehensive compilation of images of Indian war commemoration. This summary is based on personal travel and the following works: Hart, *Old Forts of the Northwest*; Herbert M. Hart, *Old Forts of the Southwest* (Seattle: Superior Publishing Co., 1964); Herbert M. Hart, *Old Forts of the Far West* (New York:

Bonanza Books, 1965); Paul L. Hedren, *Traveler's Guide to the Great Sioux War: The Battlefields, Forts, and Related Sites of America's Greatest Indian War* (Helena: Montana Historical Society Press, 1996); Steve Rajtar, *Indian War Sites: A Guidebook to Battlefields, Monuments, and Memorials, State by State with Canada and Mexico* (Jefferson, N.C.: McFarland and Co., 1999); and Robert G. Ferris, ed., *Soldier and Brave: Historic Places Associated with Indian Affairs and the Indian Wars in the Trans-Mississippi West* (Washington, D.C.: National Park Service, 1971). *See also* Mayo, *War Memorials as Political Landscape*; Foote, *Shadowed Ground*; and Andrew Hogarth and Kim Vaughn, *Battlefields, Monuments and Markers: A Guide to Native American & United States Army Engagements from 1854–1890* (Sydney, Australia: Andrew Hogarth Publishing, 1993). The Fort McPherson monument is shown in Hart, *Old Forts of the Northwest*, p. 75. Mayo notes two monuments that belong in neither the standard Indian war category or the Civil War style: one to Rough Rider Bucky O'Neill and another to the Mormon Battalion (pp. 141, 158). Hedren also cites two with the faces of major frontier personages: an obelisk with Sitting Bull's visage at the Hunkpapa chief's grave and a bas-relief of General George Crook conferring with the Apache chief Geronimo (pp. 119, 120).

12. G. Kurt Piehler, *Remembering War the American Way* (Washington, D.C.: Smithsonian Institution Press, 1995), p. 7.

13. Frank N. Schubert, *Black Valor: Buffalo Soldiers and the Medal of Honor, 1870–1898* (Wilmington, Del.: Scholarly Resources, 1997), p. 169; "Soldier Gets New Home," *Fort Huachuca Scout* (Ariz.), 15 Feb. 2007.

14. Dudley Taylor Cornish, *The Sable Arm: Black Troops in the Union Army, 1861–1869* (1956; reprinted ed., Lawrence: University Press of Kansas, 1987). In the year before the appearance of Ford's film, buffalo soldiers appeared on television and in another film. In mid-November 1959, a segment of the National Broadcasting Company's TV western series *Zane Grey Theatre* featured Sammy Davis Jr. as a black corporal in command of a small unit ordered to bring an Indian chief to a treaty signing. *The Wonderful Country* (1959), a western that starred Robert Mitchum and Julie London, also had Leroy ("Satchel") Paige in a small role as a cavalry sergeant. *Major Dundee* (1965), a Charlton Heston film, included black soldiers and was followed by a few others, including the deservedly obscure *Soul Soldier* (1970), Mario Van Peebles's *Posse* (1993), and the Danny Glover effort, *Buffalo Soldiers* (1997). *TV Guide* 7 (7 Nov. 1959): p. A59; Leonard Maltin, *Movie and Video Guide, 1996* (New York: Signet Books, 1995), pp. 808–9, 1030, 1477; Buck O'Neill, with Steve Wulf and David Conrads, *I Was Right on Time: My Journey from the Negro Leagues to the Majors* (New York: Simon and Schuster, 1996), p. 214; Darius James, *That's Blaxploitation!: Roots of the Baadasssss 'Tude (Rated X by an All-Whyte Jury* (New York: St. Martin's Griffin, 1995), p. 43. On *Sergeant Rutledge*, *see* Scott

Eyman, *Print the Legend: The Life and Times of John Ford* (New York: Simon and Schuster, 1999), p. 475.

15. Ludwig Lauerhass, "A Commemoration: The Shaw Memorial in American Culture," in *Shaw Memorial*, pp. 61–62.

16. William Leckie, *The Buffalo Soldiers: A Narrative of the Negro Cavalry in the West* (Norman: University of Oklahoma Press, 1967); D. Barnes, M. Smith, and M. Lewis, "The Buffalo Soldiers" (ca. 1969), recorded by the Persuasions on Polydor.

17. Henry Louis Gates, Jr., "Powell and the Black Elite," *New Yorker*, 25 Sept. 1995, p. 64; *New York Times*, 15 May 1994 (quotation). On the connection between Powell and the buffalo soldiers, *see also* Walter Hill, "Exploring the Life and History of the 'Buffalo Soldiers,'" *Record* (National Archives and Records Administration) 4 (Mar. 1998): 12.

18. 9th and 10th (Horse) Cavalry Association, *The Buffalo Soldier Monument Dedication* (Topeka, Kans.: Mainline Printing, 1992); Anthony Williams, "The Buffalo Soldier Monument," *Army* 47 (Feb. 1997): 61–63; Colin Powell, with Joseph E. Persico, *My American Journey* (New York: Random House, 1995), pp. 554–57. Powell's speech is quoted from Charlotte Raub, "Buffalo Soldiers—A 'First' in American Military History," *INSCOM Journal* 22 (Jan.–Mar. 1999): 29.

19. U.S., Senate, 102nd Congr., 2nd sess., Joint Resolution 92, 3 Jan. 1992; U.S., House of Representatives, 102nd Congr., 1st Sess., Joint Resolution 237, 25 Apr. 1991.

20. James N. Leiker, "Black Soldiers at Fort Hays, Kansas, 1867–1869: A Study in Civilian and Military Violence," *Great Plains Quarterly* 17 (Winter 1997): 3.

21. Patricia Erickson, "Buffalo Soldier Monument Planned," *Public History News* (National Council on Public History) 12 (Fall 1991): 1; Sandra Griffin, "Silver City Paying Tribute to Buffalo Soldier," *New Mexico Magazine* (July 1992): 31.

22. Erickson, "Buffalo Soldier Monument Planned"; "The Sentinel," *Albuquerque Journal*, 24 July 1994; Stephen Siegfried, "Buffalo Soldier History Coming to the Forefront," *Silver City Daily Press*, 17 Feb. 1996.

23. James Brooke, "Conquistador Statue Stirs Hispanic Pride and Indian Rage," *New York Times*, 9 Feb. 1998.

24. Jim Conley, "Buffalo Soldier Statue to See Duty in December," *El Paso* (Tex.) *Times*, 17 June 1998.

25. Ibid.; Schubert, *Black Valor*, p. 169; Patrick McKenna, "Forgotten Heroes: On the Trail of the Buffalo Soldier," *Airman* (July 1995): 38–43.

26. http://www.waymarking.com/waymarks/WMETWG_20_Chance_of_Flurries_CSU_Campus_Fort_Collins_CO. Navarro died in a car crash in 2017. For biographical information, *see* chrisnavarro.com (accessed 1 Oct. 2017).

27. Savage, *Standing Soldiers, Kneeling Slaves*, p. 98.

28. Kirk Savage, "The Politics of Memory: Black Emancipation and the Civil War Monument," in *Commemorations: The Politics of National Identity*, ed. John R. Gillis (Princeton, N.J.: Princeton University Press, 1996), p. 135 (quotation); Piehler, *Remembering War the American Way*, pp. 7, 182.

29. Conference Report for H.R. 3194, *Congressional Record* 145, No. 163, Pt. II (17 Nov. 1999): H12, p. 367; "Interpretation Said Shifting at National Battlefield Parks," *Headquarters Heliogram* (Council on America's Military Past), No. 280 (Sept.–Oct. 2000): 5 (quotation).

30. Allida Black, "Struggling with Icons: Memorializing Franklin and Eleanor Roosevelt: Franklin Delano Roosevelt Memorial, National Park Service, National Capitol Region," *Public Historian* 21 (Winter 1999): 72 (first three quotations); David Lowenthal, "Past Time, Present Place: Landscape and Memory," *Geographical Review* 65 (1975), quoted in Foote, *Shadowed Ground*, p. 5 (fourth quotation).

31. In 1921 a small stone marker with a bas-relief bust of Custer was unveiled at Custer Park, Hardin, Montana, about fifteen miles from the Little Bighorn Battlefield, before about 15,000 people, during the forty-fifth anniversary commemoration. The historical marker at the Washita battlefield, where Custer surprised and destroyed a peaceful Cheyenne village in 1868, has portraits of Custer and the Cheyenne leader Black Kettle. Custer also stands, saber in hand, on a monument in Custer City, Colorado, and a headstone in the cemetery at the Little Bighorn Battlefield National Monument bears his name. Other Custer monuments are at the United States Military Academy, West Point, New York, in Custer's hometown of Monroe, Michigan, and in Detroit, Michigan. A statue at Gettysburg National Military Park commemorates the contribution of his Michigan Brigade of cavalry. Custer's portrait on a bronze plaque adorns the base of the granite Gettysburg monument. Brian W. Dippie, *Custer's Last Stand: The Anatomy of an American Myth* (Lincoln: University of Nebraska Press, 1994), p. 92; Edward Tabor Linenthal, *Sacred Ground: American and Their Battlefields* (Urbana: University of Illinois Press, 1991), pp. 135, 138; Robert M. Utley, *Custer: Cavalier in Buckskin* (Norman: University of Oklahoma Press, 2001), pp. 72, 163; Smithsonian Institution Research Information System, "Inventories of American Painting and Sculpture," siris.si.edu (accessed 31 Aug. 2001).

32. Dippie, *Custer's Last Stand*, pp. 132–33.

33. Paul Andrew Hutton, "'Correct in Every Detail': General Custer in Hollywood," in *The Custer Reader*, ed. Hutton (Lincoln: University of Nebraska Press, 1992), p. 524 (quotation); Bruce A. Rosenberg, "Custer: The Legend of the Martyred Hero in America," ibid., pp. 525–47.

34. Hutton, "From Little Bighorn to Little Big Man: The Changing Image of a Western Hero in Popular Culture," in *The Custer Reader*, pp. 395–423.

35. Dippie, *Custer's Last Stand*, p. 35; Edward Tabor Linenthal, *Changing Images of the Warrior Hero in America: A History of Popular Symbolism* (New York: E. Millen, 1982), pp. 28–29; Rosenberg, "Custer."

36. *See*, for example, James Welch, with Paul Stekler, *Killing Custer: The Battle of the Little Bighorn and the Fate of the Plains Indians* (New York: W. W. Norton, 1994), pp. 61, 127, 170. Emphasizing the prowess of an enemy in order to emphasize your own is not a new phenomenon. Henry Kamen, *Empire: How Spain Became a World Power, 1492–1763* (New York: Harper Collins, 2003), pp. xxii–xxiii.

37. Dippie, *Custer's Last Stand*, pp. 4, 110 (quotation).

38. Lowenthal, "Past Time, Present Place."

39. David Lowenthal, *Possessed by the Past: The Heritage Crusade and the Spoils of History* (London: Free Press, 1997), p. 142.

40. Hutton, "From Little Bighorn to Little Big Man."

41. Schubert, *Black Valor*, pp. 128–29. On the social significance of the use of blackface, *see* David M. Blight, *Race and Reunion: The Civil War in American Memory* (Cambridge, Mass.: Belknap Press of Harvard University Press, 2001), pp. 222–31, 286.

42. Joel Kovel, *White Racism: A Psychohistory* (London: Free Association Books, 1988), pp. 211–12.

43. Quoted in Edward A. Johnson, *History of Negro Soldiers in the Spanish-American War and Other Items of Interest* (Raleigh, N.C.: Capital Printing Co., 1899), p. 34.

44. Quoted in Utley, *Custer*, p. 92.

45. Kovel, *White Racism*, p. 216.

46. Karen Needles, "Educator's Guide," learning.turner.com/Buffalo/index/html (Dec. 1997; no longer available), copy in the Frank Schubert Buffalo Soldiers Collection, SC 197, Kansas City Public Library, Kansas City, Mo.

47. On the "strangeness of the past," *see* Simon Schama, "Clio at the Multiplex," *New Yorker*, 19 Jan. 1998, pp. 38–43.

48. "U.S. Issues Buffalo Soldiers April 22," *Stamp Collector*, 26 Mar. 1994, p. 3 (first quotation); United States Postal Service, "American Commemoratives: Buffalo Soldiers," American Commemorative Panel No. 436, 1994 (second quotation).

49. Vernon Bellecourt, "The Glorification of Buffalo Soldiers Raises Racial Divisions between Blacks, Indians," *Indian Country Today* (Pine Ridge, S.Dak.), 4 May 1994.

50. *See*, for example, Cornel Pewewardy, "Buffalo Soldiers Were Federal Hired Guns," *Indian Country Today*, 23–30 June 1997.

51. *Stamp Collector*, 4, 25 June 1994; e-mail message, NATIVE-L@TAMVM1.TAMU.EDU, subject: "USPS $.50 [*sic*] stamps," 8 June 1995, copy in author's files; *Minneapolis Star Tribune*, 20 Aug. 1996; *Los Angeles Times*, 6 Feb. 1997.

52. Hutton, "From Little Bighorn to Little Big Man," p. 416.

53. "Jesolo International Sand Sculpture Exhibition," sultansofsand.com/_ww _home.html (accessed 10 Aug 2007).

John D. McDermott (center) and Thomas Buecker (second from right) stand with some of the contributors to this volume, Doug McChristian (far left), Jerome Greene (second from left), Eli Paul (third from left), and Paul Hedren (far right), at the Fort Robinson History Conference in 2013.

Appendix

Notable Works on the Frontier Army and Indian Wars by Thomas R. Buecker and John D. McDermott

THOMAS R. BUECKER

Books and Monographs

A Brave Soldier and Honest Gentleman: Lt. James E. H. Foster in the West, 1873–1881. Nebraska State Historical Society, 2013.

The Crazy Horse Surrender Ledger (with R. Eli Paul). Nebraska State Historical Society, 1994.

Fort Robinson and the American Century, 1900–1948. Nebraska State Historical Society, 2002. Reprinted by University of Oklahoma Press, 2004.

Fort Robinson and the American West, 1874–1899. Nebraska State Historical Society, 1999. Reprinted by University of Oklahoma Press, 2003.

Last Days of Red Cloud Agency: Peter T. Buckley's Photograph Collection, 1876–1877. Nebraska State Historical Society, 2016.

Articles

"'Can You Send Us Immediate Relief?': Army Expeditions to the Northern Black Hills, 1877–1878." *South Dakota History* 25 (Summer 1995): 97–115.

"Cheyenne Outbreak Firearms" (with R. Eli Paul). *Museum of the Fur Trade Quarterly* 29 (Summer 1993): 2–12.

"Confrontation at Sturgis: An Episode in Civil-Military Race Relations, 1885." *South Dakota History* 14 (Fall 1984): 238–61.

"Crazy Horse: The Search for the Elusive (and Improbable) Photo of the Famous Oglala Chief." *Greasy Grass* (Custer Battlefield Historical & Museum Association) 14 (May 1998): 27–35.

"'Distance Lends Enchantment to the View': The 1874 Black Hills Expedition Diary of Fred W. Power." *South Dakota History* 27 (Winter 1997): 197–260.

"'The Even Tenor of Our Way Is Pursued Undisturbed': Henry P. Smith's Diary during the Ghost Dance Movement, 1890–1891." *South Dakota History* 34 (Fall 2004): 197–236.

"Fort Niobrara, 1880–1906: Guardian of the Rosebud Sioux." *Nebraska History* 65 (Fall 1984): 301–26. Reprinted by Fort Niobrara Natural History Association, 1992.

"Frederic S. Calhoun: A Little Known Member of the Custer Clique." *Greasy Grass* (Custer Battlefield Historical & Museum Association) 10 (May 1994): 16–25.

"Fred W. Power, 1874 Black Hills Expedition Diarist: The Rest of the Story." *South Dakota History* 33 (Summer 2003): 180–91.

"History of Camp Sheridan, Nebraska." *Periodical: Journal of America's Military Past* 22 (1995): 55–73.

"In the Old Army: Harry K. Hollenbach at Fort Robinson, 1911–1913." *Nebraska History* 71 (Spring 1990): 16–21.

"The Journals of James S. McClellan, 1st Sgt., Co. H, 3rd Cavalry." *Annals of Wyoming* 57 (Spring 1985): 21–34.

"Letters from a Post Surgeon's Wife: The Fort Washakie Correspondence of Caroline Frey Winne, May 1879–May 1880." *Annals of Wyoming* 53 (Fall 1981): 44–63.

"Letters of Caroline Frey Winne from Sidney Barracks and Fort McPherson, Nebraska, 1874–1878." *Nebraska History* 62 (Spring 1981): 1–46.

"Lt. William Philo Clark's Sioux War Report and Little Big Horn Map." *Greasy Grass* (Custer Battlefield Historical & Museum Association) 7 (May 1991): 11–21.

"'The Men Behaved Splendidly': Guy V. Henry's Famous Cavalry Rides." *Nebraska History* 78 (Summer 1997): 54–63.

"One Soldier's Service: Caleb Benson in the Ninth and Tenth Cavalry, 1875–1908." *Nebraska History* 74 (Summer 1993): 54–62. Reprinted in *Buffalo Soldiers in the West: A Black Soldiers Anthology*, edited by Bruce A. Glasrud and Michael N. Searles, pp. 114–28. Texas A&M University Press, 2007.

"The Post of North Platte Station, 1867–1878." *Nebraska History* 63 (Fall 1982): 381–98.

"Prelude to Brownsville: The Twenty-Fifth Infantry at Fort Niobrara, Nebraska, 1902–1906." *Great Plains Quarterly* 16 (Spring 1996): 95–106.

"'Pretty Well Fixed for Defense': Enclosed Army Posts in the Northern Plains, 1819–1872." *Nebraska History* 95 (Spring 2014): 14–27.

"A Surgeon at the Little Big Horn: The Letters of Dr. Holmes O. Paulding." *Montana: The Magazine of Western History* 32 (Autumn 1982): 34–49.

JOHN D. MCDERMOTT

Books and Monographs

All Because of a Mormon Cow: Historical Accounts of the Grattan Massacre, 1854–1855 (with R. Eli Paul and Sandra J. Lowry). University of Oklahoma Press, 2018.

Circle of Fire: The Indian War of 1865. Stackpole Books, 2003.

Dangerous Duty: A History of Frontier Forts in Fremont County, Wyoming. Fremont County Historical Preservation Commission, 1993.

The Dull Knife Symposium (ed.). Fort Phil Kearny/Bozeman Trail Association, 1989.

Forlorn Hope: The Battle of White Bird Canyon and the Beginning of the Nez Perce War. Idaho State Historical Society, 1978. Reprinted as *Forlorn Hope: The Nez Perce Victory at White Bird Canyon*. Caxton Press, 2003.

Fort Mackenzie: A Century of Service, 1898–1998. Fort Mackenzie Centennial Committee, 1998.

Frontier Crossroads: The History of Fort Caspar and the Upper Platte Crossing. City of Casper, 1997.

General George Crook's 1876 Campaigns: A Report Prepared for the American Battlefield Protection Program. Frontier Heritage Alliance, 2000.

A Guide to the Indian Wars of the West. University of Nebraska Press, 1998.

Red Cloud, Oglala Legend. South Dakota Biography Series, No. 4. South Dakota State Historical Society Press, 2015.

Red Cloud's War: The Bozeman Trail, 1866–1868. 2 vols. University of Oklahoma Press, 2010.

Articles

"Crime and Punishment in the United States Army: A Phase of Fort Laramie History." *Journal of the West* 7 (Apr. 1968): 246–55.

"Custer and the Little Bighorn Story: What It All Means." In *Legacy: New Perspectives on the Battle of the Little Bighorn*, ed. Charles E. Rankin, pp. 93–111. Montana Historical Society Press, 1996.

"Fort Laramie's Silent Soldier, Leodegar Schnyder." *Annals of Wyoming* 36 (Apr. 1964): 5–8.

"The *Frontier Scout*: A View of Fort Rice in 1865." *North Dakota History* 61 (Fall 1994): 25–35.

"Introduction." In *The Bozeman Trail* by Grace Hebard and E. A. Brininstool, 2 vols. 1:1–8, 2:1–8. University of Nebraska Press, 1990.

"Introduction." In *Indian War of 1864,* by Eugene F. Ware, pp. xi–xix. University of Nebraska Press, 1994.

"Introduction." In *My Army Life: A Soldier's Wife at Fort Phil Kearny,* by Frances C. Carrington, pp. xi–xxix. Pruett Publishing Co., 1990.

"Military Command at Fort Laramie" (with Gordon Chappell). *Annals of Wyoming* 38 (Apr. 1966): 7–48.

"The Military Problem and the Black Hills, 1874–1875." In *Gold Rush: The Black Hills Story,* ed. John D. McDermott, pp. 4–26. South Dakota State Historical Society Press, 2001.

"No Small Potatoes: Problems of Food and Health at Fort Laramie, 1849–1859." *Nebraska History* 79 (Winter 1998): 162–70.

"The Plains Forts: A Harsh Environment." *Nebraska History* 91 (Spring 2010): 2–15.

"Price of Arrogance: The Short and Controversial Life of William Judd Fetterman." *Annals of Wyoming* 63 (Spring 1991): 42–53.

"'We Had a Terribly Hard Time Letting Them Go': The Battles of Mud Springs and Rush Creek." *Nebraska History* 77 (Summer 1996): 78–88.

"Were They Really Rogues?: Desertion in the Nineteenth-Century U.S. Army." *Nebraska History* 78 (Winter 1997): 165–74.

"Wounded Knee: Centennial Voices." *South Dakota History* 20 (Winter 1990): 245–98.

Contributors

Lori Cox-Paul became interested in the frontier army following several memorable trips to historic Fort Robinson, where Tom Buecker served as its longtime curator. She has given numerous presentations on topics relating to the frontier army, including "Horsing Around: Recreational Uses of Horses in the Frontier Army" and "A Frontier Army Fourth and Other Holidays," and is the co-author of *A Frontier Army Christmas*. As a museum professional and archivist, she has spent her career curating exhibits, creating educational programs, and providing access to primary source materials. Cox-Paul currently serves as the director of archival operations for the National Archives at Kansas City.

Brian W. Dippie is professor emeritus at the University of Victoria, British Columbia. A specialist in western American culture and art, he has focused on Custer's Last Stand as a popular myth and the works of George Catlin, Frederic Remington, and especially Charles M. Russell. He has most recently provided the introduction to the C. M. Russell Museum's catalog *Charles M. Russell: The Women in His Life and Art* (2018) and the afterword to *Art of the West: Selected Works from the Autry Museum* (2018).

Jerome A. Greene is retired as a research historian with the National Park Service. He is the author and/or editor of numerous books and articles related to the Indian wars of the West. His book *American Carnage: Wounded Knee, 1890* received the 2015 Spur Award for Historical Nonfiction from the Western Writers of America. His book *Morning Star Dawn: The Powder River Campaign and the Northern Cheyennes, 1876* (2003) garnered the Robert M. Utley Award of the Western History Association. His most recent publication is *Soldiering in the Shadow of Wounded Knee: The 1891 Diary of Private Hartford G. Clark, Sixth U.S. Cavalry* (2016).

Paul L. Hedren retired in 2007 after serving nearly four decades as a National Park Service historian and superintendent successively in five states. A lifelong student of the Old Army and the Indian wars of the American West, he is the author of some sixty articles and twelve books, including the award-winning *After Custer: Loss and Transformation in Sioux*

Country (2011) and *Powder River: Disastrous Opening of the Great Sioux War* (2016). His most recent book is *Rosebud, June 17, 1876: Prelude to the Little Big Horn* (2019).

Douglas C. McChristian's career with the National Park Service spanned thirty-four years, during which he served at several western military historic sites, including Forts Larned, Davis, Laramie, and Union. He also served as chief historian at Little Bighorn Battlefield, later retiring as a research historian for the Intermountain Region. His *Fort Laramie: Military Bastion of the High Plains* won the 2010 Western Writers Spur Award. His latest book, *Regular Army O!: Soldiering on the Western Frontier, 1865–1891*, garnered the 2017 John M. Carroll Award from the Little Bighorn Associates and the 2017 Best Book Award from the Custer Battlefield Historical & Museum Association.

R. Eli Paul recently retired as the head of the Missouri Valley Special Collections at the Kansas City Public Library, Kansas City, Missouri. He has published extensively on the subject of the Plains Indians, including collaborative efforts with Tom Buecker and Jack McDermott. In 2005, Paul received the Robert M. Utley Award from the Western History Association for his book *Blue Water Creek and the First Sioux War, 1854–1856* (2004). His most recent book is *Sign Talker: Hugh Lenox Scott Remembers Indian Country* (2016).

Frank N. Schubert retired in 2003 after twenty-seven years as a historian in the Department of Defense. He was a Fulbright lecturer at Babes-Bolyai University in Cluj-Napoca, Romania, in 2003–4 and has lectured in seven European countries. His latest books are *Hungarian Borderlands: From the Habsburg Empire to the Axis Alliance, the Warsaw Pact, and the European Union* (2011) and *Other Than War: The American Military Experience and Operations in the Post–Cold War Decade* (2013). He and his wife divide their time between homes in Mount Vernon, Virginia; Eagle's Nest Lake, Minnesota; and Győr, Hungary.

Index